The Radiant Child

The
Radiant Child

Thomas Armstrong

*This publication made possible with
the assistance of the Kern Foundation*

**The Theosophical Publishing House
Wheaton, Ill. U.S.A.
Madras, India / London, England**

The Theosophical Publishing House
306 West Geneva Road
Wheaton, Illinois 60189
A publication of the Theosophical Publishing House,
a department of the Theosophical Society in America.

Library of Congress Cataloging in Publication Data

Armstrong, Thomas
    The radiant child

    Bibliography: p.
    Includes index.
    1. Mysticism. 2. Children—Religious life.
IL Title
BL625.A76
ISBN 0-8356-0600-7 (pbk.)

Printed in the United States of America

A small boy is walking on a country road. He is coming home from a neighborhood party. It is early evening, cold, moonless, starlit. The North Star is bright with clear radiance. It is the star that never changes its ordered place in the heavens. Sailors steer their ships by its light. A few nights before he had dreams of a star. He stands still, looking, wondering. Yes, this is the star of his dream. It is remote, lonely, alive with its own light, unchanging in its steadfastness. It is beautiful; it creates beauty. It is his star. It is telling him something. He must listen. It is about light, about beauty. It is about something that he must do. Is it to make remote beauty real and near? He is alone—alone with the star. To it he makes his wordless promise, and a premonition of his destiny comes to him. Long afterward he put it into words: to find and to release the essential meaning of the moment of daily life so that through its portrayal it will reveal the beauty of the transpersonal life—the life of the gods; not just to make beautiful things, but to follow the spirit which is beauty and so awakens beauty in the beholder. All this is phrased as nearly as possible as he told it to me years later. He did not know then in what medium his promise might be fulfilled....All he knows was that he must keep the spark of his own being connected with the remote star of his dream and vision. Long afterward he found his own way and always, even in moments of despair he saw "this brave o'erhanging firmament, this majestical roof fretted with golden fire, and there, central, unchanging, was his own star of purpose."

Frances Wickes, The Inner World of Choice

Contents

Portions of *The Radiant Child*, sometimes in slightly altered form, have appeared in the following journals and magazines:

"The Spiritual Origins of Childhood," *Mothering*, Summer, 1984, 14-19.

"Theosophy and the Essential Nature of the Child," *The American Theosophist*, 72:6, 1984, 213-220.

"Children as Healers," *Somatics*, Fall/Winter, 1984, 15-19.

"Transpersonal Experience in Childhood," *Journal of Transpersonal Psychology*, 16:2, 1984, 207-230. © The Transpersonal Institute, reprinted by permission.

Acknowledgments

There are many individuals whom I want to thank for their encouragement and support during the development of *The Radiant Child*, a process which spanned over ten years. Thanks to Pascal Kaplan for organizing the "Child Quest" conference in Walnut Creek, California, in October, 1978. This conference, occurring as it did upon my arrival in California, served as a stimulus to my research. Many thanks to Jim Peterson whose lecture on "The Metaphysics of Child Development" at that conference showed me what was possible in this field.

Thanks to David Surrenda and Steve Scholl-Buckwald for giving me the opportunity to teach courses in transpersonal child development at John F. Kennedy University in Orinda, California. This unique teaching experience helped me consolidate my own learning about the psychic and spiritual life of the child. A special thanks to Ralph Metzner whose encouragement and support of my ideas and careful comments on early drafts were invaluable.

Many other individuals should be acknowledged for their assistance in the research of this manuscript including Joan Alpert of the C. G. Jung Institute in San Francisco, Mary Rubach of the Rudolf Steiner library at the San Francisco Waldorf School, Vern Haddick of the California Institute of Integral Studies, and Diane Choquette of the Graduate Theological Union Library in Berkeley. Thanks too to Paul Herman, Tanya Wilkinson, Miles Vich, John Welwood, John Algeo, Ann Keohane, Carl Hurwitz, Blair Tremeroux,

Tim Bost, Helen Bee, and Annette Hollander for their feedback on selected portions of the manuscript.

Several individuals need to be acknowledged for their support over the years of my own personal process in giving birth to this work. They include: Jack Canfield, Martha Crampton, Jane Leifer, Frank Barr, Alain Youell, Murshida Ivy Duce, Jack Downing, Lenore Lefer, Sylvia Delong, Sarah Wentworth, Pam Stowe, and Thomas, Nina, and Natalie Blanks-Steinberg. I would like to thank Ken Wilber for his pioneering contributions to the emerging field of transpersonal developmental psychology.

Finally many thanks to the Kern Foundation for support of my research over the past two years, to Dora Kunz and the Theosophical Society of America, and to Shirley Nicholson for her help in guiding the development of the manuscript at each step along the way.

1

The Hidden Side of Childhood

Sweet babe, in thy face
Holy image I can trace
Sweet babe, once like thee,
Thy maker lay and wept for me,

Wept for me, for thee, for all
When he was an infant small.
Thou his image ever see,
Heavenly face that smiles on thee.[1]
William Blake

In England an eight-year-old boy suddenly experiences himself as an ancient, timeless individual. In Pennsylvania a child taking holy communion for the first time sees Christ walking toward her. In Washington a girl of seven who nearly drowned describes the experience as a celestial event. In Oklahoma a Native American boy on his sickbed has a vision of healing his people, which in later years he shares with his tribe. Increasingly throughout the United States and the world, cases of unusual or *non-ordinary* experiences are being reported by children and by adults remembering their childhood. These experiences go beyond our conventional notions of "reality" and appear to defy standard principles of developmental psychology. We do not yet know how common childhood experiences of this kind are in the general population. If it turns out that they are more than isolated examples or unique aberrations of a few exceptional individuals, then the presence of these non-ordinary child-

1

hood states could radically change the way in which we think about childhood.

In the past twenty years we have learned a great deal about the deeper regions of the psyche. Through contributions in such fields as parapsychology, comparative religion, and transpersonal psychology, our understanding of consciousness has skyrocketed. The experiences of saints, healers, psychics, and shamans are increasingly being seen as instances of awareness which go far beyond our standard concepts of human capacity. Many now recognize that the potentials which are inherent in these extraordinary people are in fact abilities which are accessible by *all* human beings. Yet thus far little work has been done to discover the extent to which these levels of experience occur in childhood. In this book I will suggest childhood represents a vast storehouse of extraordinary experiences whose recognition and acceptance could signal a dramatic change in the ways in which we parent and educate children.

Emotional expressiveness, spontaneity, and imagination are well-known characteristics of childhood. However, what I am pointing to in this book goes beyond these qualities. I am suggesting that children have access to experiences which are not merely the product of fantasy, that children are capable of levels of perception into what Abraham Maslow called "the farther reaches of human nature." Most of us are inclined to think of childhood as a time when consciousness is less developed, less evolved, and more primitive than mature adult awareness. There is a great deal of support for this idea of childhood in psychological circles. The behaviorists, for example, see the newborn as a "blank slate" onto which culture can inscribe its social programs and behavioral modifications. The psychodynamic (Freudian) school sees the infant as a mass of primitive instincts which are eventually directed into a variety of socially constructive channels. One psychoanalyst, Margaret Mahler, suggested that "the infant seems to be in a state of primitive hallucinatory disorientation in which need satisfaction seems to belong to his own 'unconditional,' omnipotent, autistic orbit."² Finally, the cognitive psychologists (including Piaget), view the infant as possessing a bundle of primitive sensorimotor structures that by adolescence will eventually evolve and mature into abstract thinking.

Each of these models regards the child as developing from *less* into *more*. This of course makes sense. Anybody who has observed children will notice that the child does not possess the skills, fluency, adaptability, or control that the average adult has. I won't argue with the experts on these basic truths. What I will suggest in this book is that there is a hidden side of childhood that needs to be acknowledged as a valid dimension of the child's existence over and above what is more easily observable.

It seems that such an idea of childhood has been recognized by only a few mystics, a handful of poets, and a scattering of transpersonal psychologists. Christ's "whoever does not accept the kingdom of God like a child will never enter it" is perhaps the best-known example of this kind of recognition.³ Less well-known are Eastern affirmations of the child's divinity. Mencius noted that "the great man is he who does not lose his child's heart."⁴ Lao Tzu observed that "one who is weighty in virtue, resembles an infant child."⁵

In the Western poetic tradition, Thomas Traherne celebrated the richness of infancy in the following passage:

How like an Angel came I down!
How bright are all things here!
When first among his Works I did appear.
O how their Glory did me crown
The world resembled his ETERNITY
In which my Soul did walk;
And ev'ry thing that I did see
Did with me talk.⁶

The most famous paean of the child's inner wealth in Western poetry is William Wordsworth's "Ode: Intimations of Immortality from Recollections of Early Childhood," which includes this well-known passage:

Our birth is but a sleep and a forgetting:
The Soul that rises with us, our life's Star,
Hath had elsewhere its setting,
And cometh from afar:
Not in entire forgetfulness,
And not in utter nakedness,
But trailing clouds of Glory do we come
From God, who is our home:
Heaven lies about us in our infancy![7]

This perspective was shared by William Blake who as a child of nine experienced visions of angels and supraordinary apparitions.

Blake was beside himself with excitement when he first read the "Intimations Ode" and saw that Wordsworth also viewed the child as a "Mighty Prophet" and "Seer Blest." He would have approved also the passage in *The Prelude* where Wordsworth finds in infancy the "first poetic spirit of our human life." The presence of this faculty in the child implies its universal presence in man . . . [8]

From the poetic or mystical viewpoint, childhood is a time when perception is fresh and new, undimmed by what Ernest Schactel has called "the procrustean bed of culturally prevalent experience schemata which allow for certain experiences, forbid others, and omit a great many for which the culture has either no frame of reference or only an unsuitable one."[9] In a sense, the child possesses the "beginner's mind" of Zen.[10] Everything the infant sees, it sees for the first time, with wonder and amazement, or if it be dread, then a kind of holy dread, not unlike the "mysterium tremendum" described by Rudolf Otto in his *Idea of the Holy*.[11] According to this model, the child is *not* an immature being but has extraordinary levels of insight and deep reservoirs of inspiration and illumination.

So who is right, the behaviorists or Wordsworth? Freud or Christ? Does the child begin life in a state of disorientation or a state of divine rapture? Do young children have access to the realm of psychics and saints or are their perceptions of the world primitive and immature? I would like to

4

suggest that *both* views are correct. In order to understand how this can be true, I need to paint a twofold picture of the child. According to Geoffrey Hodson, an esoteric philosopher, "the child, like all human beings, is primarily dual: an immortal spiritual being in a mortal material body."[12] Within this context, I can begin to speak of two different dimensions or lines of development within the child. One line describes the growth of the child ultimately in biological/material terms. This strand has been very well explored and documented by contemporary developmental psychology. I call this line the development of the child *from the body up.*

I would claim that there is a second line of development which parallels, interacts with, and may even ultimately support the development of the first line of growth. This hidden line of development I call the growth of the child *from the spirit down.* Let me turn now to a description of each of these lines of development.

In the "body-up" strand of development, the child begins life as a zygote in the mother's womb (a purely biological entity presumably without consciousness). From there it grows into blastocyst, an embryo, a fetus, and ultimately into a newly born baby. At some point, either before or shortly after birth, the child begins to develop the most rudimentary consciousness which is highly fused to physical existence. In the earliest stages, the child is said to be psychologically united with the mother. That means that it cannot yet distinguish a sense of "I" and "m(other)." In the child's experience his body and the mother's body are inseparably intertwined; the child cannot tell where the one leaves off and the other begins. Ken Wilber points out the predominance of this viewpoint in modern psychology:

> Freud and the whole psychoanalytic movement, the entire Jungian tradition, the Kleinians, the modern ego psychologists such as Mahler, Loevinger, and Kaplan, and the cognitive psychologists in general—all essentially agree that the infant's first structure of consciousness is this type of material fusion consciousness. . . [13]

Gradually the child starts to form stable images of self and other, begins to establish a rudimentary ego or self-structure and evolves through sequential stages of motoric, perceptual, affective, and intellectual growth. Development along this line sees a growing adaptation to cultural norms or societal standards and an increased attention to what is agreed upon as "objective reality." It is important to stress that in this "body up" line of development, all future maturation of the child, including the highest forms of abstract reasoning, take place within the context of an initially material or biologically based matrix. As Joseph Chilton Pearce has said,

> So long as we live (or she lives), the physical mother remains the primary matrix even though we separate from her and move into larger matrices. Throughout our lives, the earth remains the matrix of all matrices. No matter how abstract our explorations of pure thought and created reality, the mind draws its energy from the brain, which draws its energy from the body matrix, which draws its energy from the earth matrix.[14]

On the other hand, what I will attempt to describe in this book is a second, complementary strand of development, a hidden line of maturation that describes the growth of the child "from the spirit down." By this I mean that there is a part of the child which does *not* have its roots in the mother or earth matrix, as Pearce has described it. There is a dimension of the child (and therefore of all of us) that has its foundations elsewhere.

Where, you might ask, is this "elsewhere"? This is a difficult question to answer adequately or clearly. I can only begin by suggesting that this question is not a new one. Some traditions have considered these origins as residing in a previous existence (past life). Other traditions have ascribed these origins to a heavenly or celestial realm. Hazrat Inayat Khan, a Sufi mystic, suggested this when he said, " . . . an infant brings with it to the earth the spirit with which it is impressed from the angelic spheres and from the plane of the jinn."[15] Other esoteric traditions have

6

talked about the infant descending from astral or mental planes of consciousness into an incarnation as a physical being. More recently Jungian psychologists have referred to the child's initial connection with the collective unconscious or the Self.

None of these philosophies denies the importance of the biological parents in creating the physical organism that becomes the child. However they imply that there is some other part of the child that exists previous even to conception (reminiscent of a famous Zen koan: "what was your original face—the one you had before your parents gave birth to you?")

This is the line of development that Wordsworth wrote about when he described the child as "trailing clouds of glory." This "spirit down" strand of growth defines the journey from a higher/broader/deeper/more comprehensive level of nonmaterial existence to a narrower/more confining/more separate/material or bodily existence. This journey has been described in various traditions as the fall from grace, the exile from Paradise, the incarnation of the soul into the body, or the imprisonment of the spirit ("shades of the Prison House begin to close in on the growing boy"[16]). What occurs during this journey may have a great deal to do with the many kinds of non-ordinary experiences that we will examine in this book.

Clearly *both* lines of development are necessary in the life of the child. Without the "body up" component, the child would not be a child. That is, the child would not have the growing physical body which is necessary for experiencing earthly existence. Many traditions agree that the taking of a birth is no accidental or idle occurrence. It creates the structures, according to some Eastern paths, through which karma or the deeds of past lives can be balanced with actions of a complementary nature. Other traditions speak of the need to learn lessons from one's earthly existence as a prerequisite for spiritual advancement: without the "body up" line of development, the child would have no way of "grounding" deeper truths. On a more psychological level, without the "body up" line of development, children would have no way of contacting and becoming part of the culture into which they have been born. On the other hand, without the "spirit down" component, the child would seem to lack some very deep dimension of the psyche that is necessary in order to give direction and coherence to the earthly journey. Without the "spirit down" element, the child would grow "up from the body" without purpose, aim, or sense of life pattern or destiny.

The "body up" line of development has been extensively described in contemporary psychology. In fact, modern child psychology is almost exclusively concerned with this aspect of the child. Pick up any textbook on child development or child psychology and you will see what I mean. These texts describe the specific stages children go through in walking, talking, seeing, hearing, feeling, socializing, thinking and performing a whole range of functions. These texts talk about the importance of prenatal care, the mother-child relationship, the importance of peer relationships, the development of language and the ways in which the child learns to make sense out of society's rules. They cover all the processes that a child goes through in becoming part of the everyday, concrete, nitty-gritty world of people, ideas, and things. These texts are carefully worked out road maps of the path that children take in making their way from a complete embeddedness in materiality. They show how children go through a series of progressively more complex, abstract, flexible and interactive stages of thought, emotion, and perception. With each advancing stage, the child more closely approximates the behavior and thought of the average adult in the culture. When this pathway is blocked, for whatever reason, these texts describe the pathology which results.

In all of this there is simply not much room left for the miraculous and the extraordinary. When the remarkable or the profound do occur in the lives of children, these contemporary systems of child psychology are likely to do one of two things with respect to them. Either they will fail to recognize such experiences, simply because their maps have no place for these phenomena, or they will reduce them to forms and shapes that can be managed within their system. Hence, "visions" will be turned into "primitive fantasies," remarkable encounters with incredible beings will be regarded as "projections of the undifferentiated psyche of the child onto the world," and so on. Freudians have tended to regard all visions as "hallucinations" or "primary process thinking." Deep religious experiences are reduced to regressions to the mother-fusion state or omnipotent images of the father.[17] Followers of Jean Piaget would tend to attribute a child's early religious fantasies or supramundane perceptions to "preoperational" cognition, a form of thinking which is considered to be confused, paradoxical, and inferior to more adult forms of reasoning.

I do not deny that children do in fact fantasize, project, regress, and perceive the world in primitive ways. That, in fact, is a large part of what childhood is all about. I will say, however, that not all visions are fantasies, not all of the child's religious experiences are primary process thinking, and not all of the child's encounters with the non-ordinary are due to primitive perception. When the child does project or fantasize, we know that we are dealing with the "body up" line of development. However, when we can ascertain that the child is actually experiencing a deep religious feeling, a genuine vision, or a supramundane perception, then we *may* be dealing with the "spirit down" strand of growth. (I say *may* because there are non-ordinary experiences that we shall deal with in this book that seem to come more from the "body up" strand of development.)

As mentioned, another reason we don't hear much about non-ordinary experiences in childhood is that up until now there simply have been no maps available through which to decipher the deeper potentialities of the child. Generally the only kinds of resources available have been those in scripture and poetry, as described above. Parents, teachers, and others who work with children have had little else to guide them. Since the culture has no room for the non-ordinary experiences, children tend to forget, repress, or in other ways deny these experiences as they move toward increasing enculturation and adaptation. Those parents who manage to stay in touch with their own intuitions about a child's deeper potentialities find that these intuitions tend to be crowded out by the overwhelming number of theories, research discoveries, and child-rearing books that ignore a child's "spirit down" perceptions. Thus on the one hand we have a body of knowledge concerning "spirit down" experience in childhood that is largely metaphorical, and on the other hand, we have a vast quantity of empirical and theoretical research in child development that is of the "body up" variety.

This book was written to begin the process of documenting the "spirit down" potentialities of the child in terms that are empirical and theoretical as well as poetic and metaphorical. I will weave together many different instances of non-ordinary experience in childhood with findings in child psychology, comparative religion, mythology, metaphysics, anthropology, literature and philosophy to create what I hope will be a foundation for further research into this dimension of the child's existence. I envision such a field exploring the child's experience of the extraordinary: visions, intuitions, ecstasies, encounters with the supernatural, confrontations with the infinite, interactions with other levels of existence and so on. Moreover, I see this field applying these findings in the lives of children by exploring ways in which children can learn to integrate rather than repress or forget such experiences as they grow up.

In the next chapter I will look at many different kinds of non-ordinary experience reported by children and by adults remembering their childhood. In subsequent chapters I will attempt to make sense out of these experiences from several different theoretical perspectives including transpersonal psychology (Chapter 3), world mythology (Chapter 4), and the ancient wisdom or esoteric science (Chapter 5). After briefly exploring the role of the child in healing (Chapter 6) I will try to reconcile traditional views of childhood with the non-ordinary experiences described in this book by suggesting that we think of childhood in terms of a spectrum of consciousness (Chapters 7 and 8). Finally, I intend to show how this approach to childhood can enrich the ways in which we work with children, whether as parents, teachers, therapists or researchers (Chapter 9) and how ultimately our vision of "the radiant child" must include the *total* child, where "body up" and "spirit down" potentialities are inextricably interwoven into a seamless unity (Chapter 10).

I hope that this adventure into the hidden side of childhood will shed light on the origins of mystical experience, religious inspiration, creativity, psychic perception and a host of related concerns. By exploring the extraordinary in childhood, I am essentially exploring the miraculous in all of us. In attempting to discover ways of integrating these experiences with our culture-bound selves, I am ultimately concerned with our personal emancipation, our collective regeneration, and even our global transformation.

2

Varieties of Non-Ordinary Childhood Experience

> *I was six when I saw that everything was God, and my hair stood up, and all that,"* Teddy said. *"It was on a Sunday, I remember. My sister was only a tiny child then, and she was drinking her milk, and all of a sudden I saw that she was God and the* milk *was God. I mean, all she was doing was pouring God into God, if you know what I mean. "*[1]
>
> J. D. Salinger, "Teddy"

According to legend one of Switzerland's most beloved saints, Niklaus von der Flue, saw a star when he was still in his mother's womb. Later he said that this star was a sign to him that he would have the opportunity to bring some light into the darkness of his times.[2] Da Free John (Franklin Jones), a well-known American spiritual leader, recalled an experience similar to that of the saint, which he said occurred during his infancy:

> As a baby I remember crawling around inquisitively with an incredible sense of joy, light and freedom in the middle of my head that was bathed in energies moving freely down from above, up, around, and down through my body and my heart. It was an expanding sphere of joy from the heart.... That awareness, that conscious enjoyment and space centered in the midst of the heart, is the "bright."[3]

Each of these accounts, one actual, one mythical, suggests the depth of experience a human being is capable of
even at the very beginnings of life. They illustrate that profound and even ultimate levels of reality are accessible to
the youngest living human.

In this chapter I will present a whole range of experiences
that are called "non-ordinary" because they do not fit into
our usual expectations, either for what a child is capable
of or, for that matter, what any individual at any age is
capable of. These experiences will be presented with a mini-
mum of interpretation. I will leave to subsequent chapters
the task of making sense of non-ordinary experiences within
psychological, metaphysical, or other theoretical contexts.

The categories I use to organize these experiences are entirely arbitrary, with much admitted overlapping. Yet this
material serves as a starting point for presenting a wealth of
information—thus far little known—concerning the hidden
side of childhood.

Profound Religious Experience

Children are not generally thought of as religious creatures,
at least in the realm of psychology. One of the earliest
psychologists to study religious experience, E. D. Starbuck,
commented that "religion is distinctively external to the
child rather than something which possesses inner significance."[4] Other researchers who followed him echoed Starbuck's downplaying of a child's inner spiritual life. J. J.
Smith writing in 1944 observed: "A child is non-religious at
birth as he is non-moral, non-aesthetic, non-thinking. He
inherits none of these qualities in functional form but acquires them gradually through experience."[5] More recently,
developmental psychologists have attempted to correlate a
child's religious development with the theories of Jean
Piaget, Erik Erikson, and Lawrence Kohlberg.[6] The conclusion that most of these studies reach is that children's

religious understanding is limited by their cognitive, emotional, and social levels of growth.

This perspective, while accurate in describing religious development "from the body up," fails to recognize that children are capable of deep religious experiences as they come "down from the spirit." St. Catherine of Siena had her first vision of Christ at the age of six, a glimpse of eternity that was to change her life.[7] At around the age of nine William Blake had a vision of "bright angelic wings bespangling every bough like stars."[8] More recently, John Lilly, noted dolphin researcher, reported a deep religious experience which had occurred to him when he was seven and was remembered during a psychedelic session:

> I was kneeling, facing the alter [in a Catholic church], there was a single candle lighted on the altar and the rest of the church was darkened, with very little light coming in from the outside since the windows were high up. Suddenly the church disappeared, the pillars were shadowy, and I saw angels, God on His Throne and the saints moving through the church in another set of dimensions. Since I was only seven years old and had seen paintings of artistic concepts of God, this is what I saw in the visions. I also saw His love, His caring, and His creation of us.[9]

A New Jersey psychiatrist, Annette Hollander, conducted studies with a group of parents whom she described as "unchurched" (no longer affiliated with any particular religious tradition). Eighty-eight percent of the adults in her survey indicated having had mystical experiences or a feeling of the presence of something sacred or holy during their lives. Dr. Hollander indicates that many of these experiences began in childhood (she doesn't specify exactly how many). Dr. Hollander published the results of her questionnaire in a wonderful book entitled *How to Help Your Child Have a Spiritual Life*. Here is an example of a typical response from her questionnaire:

> I had these incredible mystical experiences as an Altar Boy singing from ages 4-5 until 13-14. I remember most vividly when I was 10. I figured everyone was having it.[10]

Finally, a subject in my own informal research recollected the following religious experience while attending mass:

> I was looking forward to my first holy communion because that's when Christ came into you. It was around that time that I was at mass praying at the altar. I was looking at the altar and all of a sudden I went into—I hesitate to say a trance—but all of a sudden instead of the church and the altar being there, there was a meadow filled with flowers and Christ was walking toward me in the meadow. I don't know how long it lasted, but it felt very real.[11]

Each of these experiences included symbols and settings which were explicitly religious in nature. Of course it is possible that these children were simply impressionable and appropriated the cultural trappings of their religion in a primitive or "magical" way. John Lilly responds to this argument by making the observation about his own early experience:

> One could put down the child of seven and say that he had been fed programs of the visions of saints, of Saint Theresa of Avila, that the mystical aspects of the Catholic Church had been thoroughly programmed into this young man and that he was projecting his visions totally. I then remember that I had made the mistake of confiding in a nun that I had had this vision. She was horrified and said that only saints had visions, putting me down thoroughly. At that point, I repressed the memory and that kind of experience, but before I repressed it I was angry, "so she doesn't think I'm a saint."[12]

Peak Experiences

Abraham Maslow coined the term "peak experience" to describe "the most wonderful experience or experiences of your life; happiest moments, ecstatic moments, moments of rapture."[13] While some of the experiences he studied had religious content, many others did not and occurred in a variety of nonreligious settings: walks in nature, being in love, reading a wonderful book, viewing a painting, engaging in creative work. Almost all of the research that has been conducted in the area of peak experience has been restricted to adults, presumably because children are not considered mature enough for these high levels of rapture. Yet once again, childhood can be a time of incredible ecstasy. Consider for example, the childhood experience of Ramakrishna, a nineteenth century Bengali saint:

> One day in June or July [Ramakrishna was six or seven years old], when he was walking along a narrow path between paddy-fields, eating the puffed rice that he carried in a basket, he looked up at the sky and saw a beautiful, dark thunder-cloud. As it spread, rapidly enveloping the whole sky, a flight of snow-white cranes passed in front of it. The beauty of the contrast overwhelmed the boy. He fell to the ground, unconscious, and the puffed rice went in all directions. Some villagers found him and carried him home in their arms. Gadadhar [Ramakrishna] said later that in that state he had experienced an indescribable joy.[14]

The chief disciple and successor to Sri Aurobindo, known as the Mother to her followers, experienced light during her childhood meditations:

> She used to sit quiet in a small chair with a little back specially made by her parents for her, and she would experience as she meditated the descent of a great brilliant Light upon her head producing a turmoil inside her brain. She had the feeling that the Light was continually growing in length and size, and she wished it would possess her completely.[15]

Jean Houston, a contemporary psychologist and pioneer of the consciousness movement in the United States, tells a loving and humorous tale of her quest at the age of six to discover the mysteries of religion. After a period of intense search, interrupted by much good-natured ribbing from her light-hearted father, Houston reported having a peak experience:

16

> . . . suddenly the key turned and the door to the universe opened. I didn't see or hear anything unusual. There were no visions, no bursts of light. The world remained the same. And yet everything around me, including myself, moved into meaning. Everything—the fig tree in the yard, the dogs in the closet, the wall safe, the airplane in the sky, the sky itself, and even my idea of the Virgin Mary— became part of a single Unity, a glorious symphonic resonance in which every part of the universe was a part of and illuminated every other part, and I knew that in some way it all worked together and was very, very good.[16]

Such experiences are not restricted to saints and psychologists. Similar reports were collected from a cross section of the British population in a study conducted by the Religious Experience Research Unit of the Alister Hardy Research Centre at Manchester College, Oxford. The research began with the placing of an advertisement in several public newspapers asking "all readers who felt that their lives had in any way been affected by some power beyond themselves" to write an account of their experience. Fifteen percent of the respondents referred back to childhood for their experiences. These individuals were then sent a questionnaire to complete, and the results were tabulated and presented in a remarkable book entitled *The Original Vision* by Edward Robinson. Here is one example of a peak experience from that study:

> The most profound experience of my life came to me when I was very young—between four and five years old . . . . My mother and I were walking on a stretch of land in Pangbourne Berks, known locally as "the moors." As the sun declined and the slight chill of evening came on, a pearly mist formed over the ground . . . . Suddenly I seemed to see the mist as a shimmering gossamer tissue and the harebells, [flowers], appearing here and there, seemed to shine with a brilliant fire. Somehow I understood that this was the living tissue of life itself, in which that which we call consciousness was embedded: appearing here and there was a shining focus of energy in that more diffused whole. In that moment I knew that I had my own special

place, as had all other things, animate and so-called inanimate, and that we were all part of this universal tissue
which was both fragile yet immensely strong and utterly
good and beneficent. The vision has never left me. It is as
clear today as fifty years ago, and with it the same intense
feeling of love of the world and the certainty of ultimate
good.[17]

Compare these childhood experiences with some of the
adult experiences of "cosmic consciousness" studied by
William James and Richard Maurice Bucke around the turn
of the century:

A sense of being bathed in a warm glow of light.[18]
Earth, heaven, and sea resounded as in one vast world-
encircling harmony.[19]
My physical body went through the experience of a disap-
pearance in spiritual light.[20]

Clearly there *is* enough similarity between these descriptions and some of the passages cited above to warrant a
closer look at the potential depths and heights of childhood
experience.

Near-Death Experiences

Since the publication in 1975 of *Life After Life* by Raymond
Moody, the study of near-death experiences has grown con-
siderably.[21] Medical doctors, nurses, psychologists, and
psychiatrists are increasingly becoming aware of individuals
who have clinically "died" on the operating table or in an
accident, and who have subsequently on recovery reported
a whole range of otherworldly phenomena experienced during the time of "death." These experiences have included
encounters with deceased relatives, friends, guardian
spirits, religious deities, trips through dark tunnels and
visions of celestial lights. As with peak experiences, this
research has been conducted predominately with adults.
However, a few studies have begun to appear that examine
near-death experiences (NDE's) in children. One recent case
of a seven-year-old Mormon girl's near-drowning was re-

ported in a recent issue of *The American Journal of Diseases of Children:*

> The patient said that the first memory she had of her near-drowning was "being in the water." She stated, "I was dead. Then I was in a tunnel. It was dark and I was scared. I couldn't walk." A woman named Elizabeth appeared, and the tunnel became bright. The woman was tall, with bright yellow hair. Together they walked to heaven. She stated that "heaven was fun. It was bright and there were lots of flowers." She said that there was a border around heaven that she could not see past. She said that she met many people, including dead grandparents, her dead maternal aunt, and Heather and Melissa, two adults waiting to be reborn. She then met the "heavenly Father and Jesus," who asked her if she wanted to return to earth. She replied, "no." Elizabeth then asked her if she wanted to see her mother. She said yes and woke up in the hospital.[22]

While some of the child's experiences were in accord with her religious background and training, several elements were not and seem consistent with reports of adult near-death experiences as reported in the literature.

Another recent study by Nancy Evans Bush reported in *Anabiosis: The Journal for Near-Death Studies* reviewed seventeen instances of near-death experience in childhood. Evans noted that certain characteristic elements of the experience (including light, a sense of well-being, and separation from the body) were more frequently encountered in childhood than in adult NDEs, based on her limited sample. One example reported from the study was of a four-year-old girl descending the cellar stairs with a flashlight to examine a burned-out lightbulb. Now an adult, this individual recollected:

> As I started to take the first step down, I flashed the beam of light up at the light bulb, curious to see if a burned-out bulb looked "burned." I stepped out and fell into the darkness. The next thing I was aware of, was being up near the ceiling over the foot of the stairs. The light was dim and at first I saw nothing unusual. Then I saw myself lying, face down, on the cement, over to the side of the stairway. I

was a little surprised, but not at all upset at seeing myself that way. I watched and saw that I didn't move at all. After a while, I said to myself, "I guess I'm dead." But I felt good! Better than I ever had. I realized I probably wouldn't be going back to my mother, but I wasn't afraid at all . . . . I noticed the dim light growing slowly brighter. The source of light was not in the basement, but far behind and slightly above me. I looked over my shoulder into the most beautiful light imaginable. It seemed to be at the end of a long tunnel which was gradually getting brighter and brighter and more and more of the light entered it. It was yellow-white and brilliant, but not painful to look at even directly. As I turned to face the light with my full "body," I felt happier than I ever had before or have since. Then the light was gone. I felt groggy and sick, with a terrible headache. I only wanted my mother, and to stop my head from hurting.[23]

At times, a child's encounter with grave illness seems to provoke miraculous healing powers from a spiritual source. In his book *Autobiography of a Yogi*, Paramahansa Yogananda told of being stricken with a life-threatening disease when he was a child of eight. As he lay near death, his mother begged him to look at a picture of Lahiri Mayasaya, a spiritual master revered by the family:

I gazed at his photograph and saw there a blinding light enveloping my body and the entire room. My nausea and other uncontrollable symptoms disappeared; I was well. At once I felt strong enough to bend over and touch Mother's feet in appreciation of her immeasurable faith in her guru.[24]

When nine years old Black Elk, the great Native American spiritual leader, was afflicted with a mysterious illness that made his arms and legs swell up and brought him close to death. At that time he had an apocalyptic vision reminiscent of St. Paul's revelations. He saw himself flying on horseback to a council of his Grandfathers. The elders gave him instruction and magical aids with which to help his people. At one point, Black Elk said that he stood "on the highest mountain of them all and round about beneath me was the whole hoop of the world." After a long series of adventures in this other realm, Black Elk returned to the tent where his sick body lay. He soon recovered and grew up to share his vision with his people and the world.[25]

Archetypal Experience

In one sense, nearly all of a child's early experience is archetypal in nature. Young children inhabit a world that is larger than life. From the vantage point of development "from the body up," the child experiences distortions of "self" and "other" that can make kings out of fathers and castles out of garden shacks. However, there seems to be a realm, as well, which is archetypal for the child in a deeper sense and which often surfaces in dreams. Here, for example, is the archetypal dream of a young girl who was undergoing Jungian therapy:

> I was on a beach with my nurse, only she wasn't there. A big wave came in and I ran away. When I came back, there were lots and lots of things on the beach and lots and lots of starfish, but one starfish was a *blue* starfish and he had an eye right in the middle of him, and he looked at me and he knew me—me-myself, I mean, and he was my starfish because he knew me-myself. So I took him home. And then I woke up.[26]

Carl Jung called this kind of dream a "big dream." He meant by this a dream which consisted of universal symbols that are cosmic in scope. In this particular dream the blue starfish can be seen as a special symbol of the child's own inner being, who was aware not merely of "me" (the child's small ego) but of "me-myself" (the deeper and more all-encompassing Self). The child, while certainly not comprehending the Jungian interpretation of the dream symbolism, shows that she possesses an awareness of something larger within her which is universal or spiritual in nature. This kind of experience is subtler than the peak experiences described above, but nevertheless it can be profound in its essential character and in its transformative effect.

Philosophical Wisdom

Most of the reports of childhood mystical experience reported thus far in this chapter have come from adults remembering what happened to them as children. This has advantages insofar as adults are able to articulate an experience in a way that a child would be hard pressed to imitate. Yet this source of information obviously has its drawbacks as well. Adults may not accurately remember their earliest experiences, or perhaps they seek to make them into something more than they actually were. After all, one could argue, how is it really possible for an adult to put into words what happened at a time in life when there were few words and concepts? We have to acknowledge that our memories can change through the years and that we might be tempted to weave into our recollections things that happened to us later in our lives.

Children may not possess the extensive vocabulary or conceptual framework of adults. However, it appears that they are more than able to express their deepest spiritual concerns. In a sense, without an adult's verbosity, children are able to put into the most elementary language what are very simple experiences. "Out of the mouth of babes, thou has founded thy strength."[27] This well-known phrase testifies, at least metaphorically, to the innocent wisdom that is spoken by a young child. There is more than metaphor, however, in many a child's reports of deeper realities. Sometimes this wisdom comes out in the course of the child's innocent questioning about life's great mysteries, as witnessed for example in this dialogue between grandmother and grandchild as related by C. G. Jung:

Granny, why are your eyes so dim?
Because I am old.
But you will become young again?
Oh dear, no. I shall become older and older, and

then I shall die.
And what then?
Then I shall be an angel.
And then you will be a baby again?

Jung comments that in the child's response "lie the seeds of the reincarnation theory which, as we know, is still alive in millions of human beings."[28]

At times this wisdom is apparent as children come up against the hypocrisy or shallowness of their culture, as in this example of a child's early religious education:

> I was sent to Sunday school and later to church . . . each week, but found it tedious . . . . The "miserable sinner" aspect of orthodox religion had a large influence on my thinking between the ages of five and nine. I hated it, and felt more and more strongly that it somehow blasphemed against the beauty, light, and all-embracing fusion of God, man, and matter which I thought I saw all around me. To my shame, at the age of nine, I leapt up in the church service, unable to bear the "for there is no health in us" intoning any longer, and shouted that God wasn't like that at all: that he was nearer than one's own hand. And I was hustled out in floods of tears.[29]

Perhaps the most powerful and moving instance of a child's deep knowing comes through in the lives of dying children. Elisabeth Kübler-Ross in her book *On Children and Death* shares the story of Edou, a seven-year-old Santa Barbara youngster stricken with leukemia from the age of three, who shared his wisdom about life, death, and the hereafter to any who would listen. Here are some excerpts from a tape that he asked to be made when he was six years old:

> *Volunteer:* Why have you decided that you want to die?
> *Edou:* Because I'm so sick . . . . When you are dead, your spirit is in heaven, and you don't have all your aches and pains anymore. Sometimes if you want to, you can come back into a healthy life where you won't have any more aches and pains . . . .

23

> *Volunteer:* Do you believe in reincarnation?
> *Edou:* Yes I do.
>
> . . .
>
> *Volunteer:* Edou, can you tell us what you think heaven looks like? Have you seen it, and do you remember what the other side looks like?
> *Edou:* No, but I think I can give you an exact sample of what it looks like. It's sort of like . . . if you went through another passageway . . . you walked right through a wall to another galaxy or something. It's sort of like walking into your brain. And it's sort of like living on a cloud, and your spirit is there but not your body. You've left your body. It really is like walking through a wall . . . walking into your mind.
> *Volunteer:* What can you tell people . . . who think this is all the life you're ever going to get? They think you only get one life and that will be it.
> *Edou:* They are wrong about that, because I will come back again.[30]

Shortly after his seventh birthday, he ordered his own medical treatment stopped and died peacefully with a smile on his face.

The Non-Ordinary in Children's Art

The arts represent a powerful way through which children can express unseen realities. Violet Madge in her book *Children in Search of Meaning* includes selections of poetry that have a "numinous" or awe-instilling quality to them. Here, for example, are the poetic inspirations of a seven-year-old girl:

> One morning in
> lark song I heard a lovely
> tone, The dark was
> gowing the sun was coming.
>
> One night very early, still light
> Two loveing Doves came flying

> To give spirit to everyone
> As they flew we saw them
> From our window.[31]

Whether the child is writing about experiences that actually happened to her or is simply fantasizing, we will never know. But the way in which she has expressed the images in her poems indicates a spiritual sensitivity beyond her years.

Painting and drawing are wonderful media for the child's expression of inner experience. In a certain sense these media are preferable to talking or writing in describing inner spiritual life because they are nonverbal ways of relating unutterable revelations. For very young children they are often the primary means of expressing inner worlds. Rhoda Kellogg, a San Francisco art educator, conducted a comprehensive study of young children's drawings and discovered that among the first recognizable forms that emerge from a child's paint brush or drawing implement are mandala-shaped circles and crosses.[32] Michael Fordham, a Jungian psychoanalyst, used these findings as a way of pointing out the young child's attunement with the wholeness of the Self.[33]

As children become older, transpersonal symbols become more rare and infrequently appear amid the more prosaic images that are a product of the emerging stages of the child's developing ego. However in the art work of certain children, transpersonal symbols can be more pronounced. For example, in a child development class that I taught some time ago, Gloria Simoneaux, an art therapist at the Children's Cancer Research Center in San Francisco, did a moving presentation of the art work of children facing catastrophic illness. Many of the paintings dealt with the pain, uncertainty, fear, and anger of these children in their battle against cancer. Other paintings revealed transformative symbols. One painting was of a bright multicolored airplane that was shaped like a rainbow. Another showed a simple pink butterfly winging its way toward the sun. Rainbows—symbols of transition as well as integration—

25

were particularly frequent as an image in many of these paintings.

Deep Intuitive Insights

Developmental psychologists observe that children pass through specific stages in their understanding of themselves and the world. Frequently this passage from one stage to another is accompanied by insights or revelations concerning a new way of thinking. While psychologists have dedicated a great deal of effort toward describing each stage in detail, they have neglected the child's own experience of inner awakening to each new stage. At times, these transformations border on deep intuitive insight. One adult reflects on such a moment in her early life:

> We were walking home along the pavement. I became spontaneously aware that each step I took decreased the way between me and my destination by precisely the same amount as it increased the distance between me and my point of departure. I had not sufficient command of language to tell anyone. It was perhaps the most thrilling and significant thing that has ever happened to me . . . . For years I tried to put it into words . . . . There was something there to do with perfection, a perfect conjunction of increasing and decreasing . . . . And when I was 15, the formulation came, in a history lesson, and I let out a great shout of joy, and was duly reprimanded.[34]

For another child, this sudden insight had more to do with language development:

> Until I was seven, religion was purely external, expressed perhaps by the nursery jingle, "one, two, three, four, five, six, seven, All good children go to Heaven," reinforced by hymns of the infant school, such as "All things bright and beautiful," "There is a green hill," etc. Then in Standard II of a Wesleyan School [in England] I had an extraordinarily vivid insight which is absolutely beyond description but which has remained with me ever since as an abiding spiritual experience. The teacher was explaining

> that in addition to common nouns and proper nouns there were also abstract nouns, which mostly ended in "-ness," such as goodness, badness, etc.; also a number of short but very important words such as love, hate, etc. It was at this point that I seemed to grow up mentally.[35]

These experiences seem consistent with "up from body" psychologies. They occur at ages which are associated with passage from one cognitive stage to another. However, they also share elements from the "spirit down" line of development in terms of the depths of excitement and the transformative impact that these events had upon later life. It could be that these moments represented a significant interface between "body up" and "spirit down" development.

Other deep insights seem to belong much more, however, to the "spirit down" world of the child, as in the following example:

> During the year when I was 8 . . . as I stood dressed to go out on one of those interminable and awful walks through the country lanes, I was actually thinking and considering my position, something like this—"Here am I, a little boy of seven; I wonder where I was eight years ago." At that tremendous thought I stood rooted to the carpet (remember I was alone in the room) with a wave of tremendous feeling sweeping over me. I suddenly felt old and aware of being somebody very ancient, weighed by Time, of almost unbeginning individuality. Eight years ago, thought I, why not eighty or eight hundred? I felt ancient and old and full of Time. Nowadays, of course, I cannot find the wording to state clearly what I mean. I remember it quite exactly, nevertheless.[36]

Psychic Perceptions

I could not conclude this chapter without taking a look at the world of psychic experience in childhood. Recently some attention has been focused in the popular media on the abilities of children to bend spoons, foretell the future, and perform other psychic feats. Popular fiction, the cinema, and television have picked up on the occult potentialities of children, and, true to form, have frequently exploited this theme by portraying children as "demon seeds" wrecking havoc on man and nature with their supernatural powers.

Clearly, most of these psychic events are quite different from those experiences that have been described above. There is a world of difference between a child who has a glimpse of eternity and a child who starts fires through psychokinesis! Yet because they are non-ordinary experiences, they need to be included in this volume. Hopefully, later chapters will begin to make sense out of the ways in which these experiences can be differentiated from the other forms of non-ordinary experience described in this chapter.

The field of psychic studies or *parapsychology* is a complex and multifaceted area of study. It includes several kinds of abilities including telepathy (the ability to "read minds"); precognition (the ability to foretell the future); clairvoyance (the ability to see invisible energies, entities, forms, etc.); and psychokinesis (the ability to affect material objects through "thought force"). While most of the formal research in these areas has been conducted with adults, there is a small but growing body of literature and experience concerned with the psychic child.

Telepathy: Beginning in the 1930s, parapsychologists conducted experiments designed to test children's abilities to pick up on the thoughts of others while these "senders" concentrated on pictures, colors, or symbols. Many experiments of this kind conducted over the last fifty years have involved interactions between students and teachers. Several of these studies suggest that extrasensory perception (ESP) is more likely to occur when there is a favorable classroom relationship (e.g. when the teacher likes the student and/or vice versa).[37] Individual researchers have also studied spontaneous occurrences of telepathy between parent and child. Berthold Schwartz, a psychiatrist, kept a diary of possible telepathic episodes occurring in the daily life of his family (which included his wife, Ardis, and their two children, Lisa and Eric). A sample entry from his diary reads:

August 12, 1960, Friday, 4:30 p.m. While feeding Lisa green pea soup, Ardis's mind wandered to a friend's remark about birthday parties and how much one should pay for a present. At that point Lisa asked, "How much does the pea cost?"[38]

Jan Ehrenwald, another psychiatrist, suggested that ESP represents a natural symbiotic link between mother and child in the child's earliest years. Telepathy could exist as a primitive means of communicating basic survival needs since the infant has not yet developed the ability to use language to accomplish these aims.[39]

Precognition: A child's psychic openness can extend to thoughts about the future. Several spontaneous cases of this kind were reported in a study conducted in India. One child stated:

> This event happened when I was sitting in my house and the idea came to me that my maternal uncle was involved in an accident and had died. A telegram was received the same evening intimating the death of my uncle. This happened at a long distance from here, when my uncle was driving a taxi over a bridge.[40]

Another child experienced this phenomenon in a dream:

> When I was at Agra, I had an intimate girl friend. When I came to Gorakhpur, I once saw in a dream that my friend had fallen from a roof and had died. After a few days her mother sent me a letter informing me that my friend Leela was dead. Then I knew that my dream had come true.[41]

Elisabeth Kübler-Ross shares a child's spiritually precognitive dream in *On Children and Death*. One morning a four-year-old girl excitedly told her mother that she had seen and talked with Jesus during the night and that Jesus had said she would be able to go up and live with him soon. Her mother had never seen the child so excited and full of energy. The child's expectations were soon fulfilled, for that afternoon she was murdered by drowning.[42]

Clairvoyance: Individuals who can "see" forms, objects, colors, and the like which are either hidden or invisible to the naked eye are said to possess clairvoyant abilities. Parapsychologists have conducted studies with child subjects who are instructed to "guess" what symbols are printed on cards hidden in envelopes. In one such study children were divided into "sheep" and "goats" depending upon whether they felt in advance such a task to be possible ("sheep") or impossible ("goats"). It was discovered that the sheep scored well above chance levels in correctly guessing the symbols, while the goats scored slightly below chance.[43]

A study of spontaneous clairvoyance in childhood was conducted by James Peterson, a Northern California elementary school teacher.[44] As part of his research, Peterson interviewed children in his classes who reported seeing colors and lights, both in the air and around human bodies. Several of the children in his survey drew pictures of what they saw.[45] Many of the children in Peterson's survey independently reported seeing the same phenomena. In some cases children would co-operate in describing the shape, colors, and movements of an energy form. Here, for example, are some remarks of two children describing energies they saw while they observed their teacher meditating:

John: We saw a white light sort of here on your face . . .

Peter: . . . right about on the nose.

John: We see blue over your eyes.

Peter: It looks like you have mascara on . . . . I see blue under his nose.

John: And your hair was blue.

Peter: Uh huh.

John: There's blue all under your chin.

Peter: He's turning something . . .

John: I know, like bluish-green.

Peter: We also see blue on his ears.
[Whispering]

John: His nose is all red.

Peter: Uh huh. There's blue, sort of, on his cheeks. We see . . .
[Whispering]

John: There are white bumps—not bumps—but like lightning coming out of the wrists.

Peter: White lights are coming out of the wrists . . . out

of little holes. The middle of his hand [palm] is blue.

John: And his mustache is pink.[46]

While it is certainly possible that the children were in collusion and attempting to deceive, it is also possible that they were in fact seeing something that modern science is only beginning to acknowledge: the presence of interpenetrating layers of energy in our world which exist in the interstices between objective and subjective experience and which interact with the "known" world of physical matter.[47]

Psychokinesis: The ability of children to control physical matter through "thought control" has been highlighted in the press through the life of the well-known adolescent psychic Matthew Manning whose autobiography *The Link* details his own precocious development in this area.[48] Psychokinesis in childhood was also publicized during Uri Geller's television broadcasts in England in 1973. Apparently Geller's television demonstration of his ability mentally to mend broken watches and bend spoons inspired hundreds of suggestible children. The network was soon beseiged by a torrent of letters sharing spontaneous cases of children performing the same feats.[49]

Joseph Chilton Pearce, author of *Magical Child*, suggested that psychokinesis develops within a child at around the age of seven with the onset of "reversibility thinking" or "the ability of the mind to entertain any state in a continuum of possible states as equally valid and return to the point from which the operation of mind begins."[50] This quality of mind, according to Pearce, is a fertile and potentially powerful tool in the life of a child. It is between the ages of seven and fourteen that the child's immense suggestibility interfaces with his ability to operate upon or interact with the concrete world. Our culture generally places limitations on what a person can and cannot do, which is why we do not see more children performing these kinds of deeds. When children in the elementary years are shown new possibilities (such as Geller's spoon-bending feat) they sometimes apparently have the capacity to "buy in" to this ability and replicate it.

31

With the onset of adolescence, a new kind of psycho-kinetic feature emerges: poltergeist phenomena. These mischievous "invisible spirits" have been known to play havoc with the contents of a adolescent's home environment, knocking books off shelves, crashing lamps into walls, or creating sudden explosions. Parapsychologists who have researched instances of these phenomena have discovered that they seem to occur in environments where an adolescent is experiencing a deep need to rebel but due to a variety of psychological, social, or cultural reasons cannot directly express that need. According to a parapsychological view, this submerged energy is released psychically as poltergeist phenomena.[51]

Making Sense of Non-Ordinary Childhood Experience

This chapter has presented a wide range of childhood experiences which cannot easily or completely be explained by conventional models of child development. As we noted in Chapter 1, the predominating schools of thought in the Western world would call many of these experiences "delusions," "hallucinations," "fantasies," or "magical thinking." Strong evidence exists, however, to suggest that there is more than childish imagination involved in many of these examples. Hence, we must either stretch existing models to make room for non-ordinary experiences or explore alternative models that can more comfortably accommodate them. In this book I have chosen the latter approach. In the next three chapters I consider these non-ordinary experiences from the vantage point of transpersonal psychology, comparative mythology, and metaphysics. Then in Chapter 8 I will attempt to create my own descriptive model for differentiating among varieties of both ordinary and non-ordinary experience in childhood. By presenting these models, I hope to open the door to further research which can begin to make greater sense of the storehouse of experience embedded within the child's psyche.

3

The Child as Self: A Psychological Approach

I felt compassion not only for the infant who was me, but for my mother and indeed everyone in the delivery room. It was as though I was leaving a beautiful, brightly-lit place where many things were open to me, to come down into a very closed and puzzling environment. It seemed as though I knew all of the troubles that lay ahead, and I felt that it was such a waste that we humans don't understand. [1]

Hypnotically regressed subject

In regression experiments conducted in San Diego by David Chamberlain, a clinical psychologist, mother and offspring were independently regressed through hypnosis to the time of the child's birth, with startling results. In many instances (reported in Chamberlain's *Consciousness at Birth: A Review of the Empirical Evidence*) mother and child gave very similar versions of the birth event. For example:

Mother: Michele was born very fast and they had to cut the cord off of her neck. People were still putting drapes on my legs even while she was being born.

Child: There is something bright, something big right over me. It's getting colder. I feel hands touching my neck, taking something off. [2]

Two daughters gave accurate descriptions of their mothers' hair styles at the time. Another mother, who described herself as drunk and disoriented by anesthetics, found her report corroborated by her child who observed, "My mother's really, really nervous, but she's not all there, seems like.[3]

Newborns are not supposed to possess the attention to detail or sensitivity to environmental factors that these reports suggest.[4] Physicians say that a newborn's neurons have not sufficiently myelinated (been insulated) to permit effective conduction of nerve impulses necessary for clear perception and memory, to say nothing of the higher cognitive skills that seem to be present in the birth accounts of these children.[5] How could these memories exist?

It may be that medical doctors are correct, that such memories are impossible according to developmental psychobiology (a "body up" perspective). However, such memories may have validity when seen from a "spirit down" vantage point. It may be that these memories are possible because the infant possesses another "point of view," as it were, above and beyond the "blooming, buzzing confusion" that William James termed the newborn's typical state of consciousness.[6]

In this chapter I will begin to explore this more mature consciousness within the psyche. Many psychological schools discount the possibility of newly born children possessing mature outlooks (remember behaviorism's "blank slate," Piaget's "material self," and Freud's narcissism from Chapter 1). However, there are psychological paradigms that *can* help to explain this phenomenon. In addition, these paradigms can help to make sense out of the varieties of non-ordinary experience described in the last chapter. These paradigms can be found within the field of transpersonal psychology. It is to this world view that I now turn.

Transpersonal Psychology—A Brief Overview

Transpersonal psychology has been called the "fourth force" in contemporary psychology.[7] It emerged out of the need to address areas of the psyche that had been neglected by mainstream psychological traditions. According to Anthony

Sutich, a pioneer of the transpersonal movement, these areas include:

> . . . unitive consciousness, meta-needs, peak experiences, ecstasy, mystical experience, being, essence, bliss, awe, wonder, transcendence of self, spirit, sacralization of everyday life, oneness, cosmic awareness, cosmic play, individual and species-wide synergy, the theories and practices of meditation, spiritual paths, compassion, transpersonal cooperation, transpersonal realization, and actualization. . .[8]

Although as a modern professional movement it is only fifteen years old, the roots of transpersonal psychology are deeply embedded in Eastern and Western religion, philosophy, and mythology. Its contemporary psychological beginnings go back as far as William James, whose studies in consciousness and religious experience are still considered relevant to current trends in the field. The first individual to use the word *transpersonal* (actually the German equivalent—*überpersönliche*) was Carl Jung, whose definition was broadly construed to refer to unconscious contents and processes beyond the boundaries of the ego or conscious personality.[9]

Transpersonal psychology as a professional field came into being in the 1960s when Abraham Maslow and Anthony Sutich concluded that the humanistic psychology movement, which they had also helped to found, was not comprehensive enough to include all that was being discovered about "the farther reaches of human nature." Originally termed "trans-humanistic," the field of transpersonal psychology was officially born with the publication in 1969 of the *Journal of Transpersonal Psychology*.[10] The field grew rapidly with the founding of the Association for Transpersonal Psychology in 1971 and the first of its annual conferences in 1973. In 1972 the International Transpersonal Association was founded and has conducted conferences in Iceland, India, Finland, Brazil, Switzerland, Australia, and the United States.

The Radiant Child

The transpersonal perspective gained increasing recognition with the publication of numerous books and articles that applied its perspective to a wide range of disciplines. It continues to grow as scholars, researchers, psychotherapists, spiritual practitioners, and individuals from all walks of life find common ground in its approach to human experience.

The transpersonal world view helps make sense of non-ordinary experiences in childhood. In showing how it does this, I will draw upon four transpersonal thinkers: Carl Jung, Roberto Assagioli, John Welwood, and Ken Wilber. While these four theorists share common assumptions about the nature of reality, there are also many important differences among them. Each has a unique psychological perspective to lend to the discussion of non-ordinary childhood experience.

Carl Jung and the Concept of Self

Carl Jung is one of the pre-eminent psychological figures of the twentieth century. Beginning his career as the "heir" to Freud's psychoanalytic empire, Jung soon departed from Freud's rigid adherence to a sexual basis for psychopathology and developed a unique and creative psychology—called analytical psychology—which reflects not only Western psychological concepts but also owes a great deal to Western and Eastern religious, philosophical, and mythological sources.

Perhaps Jung's most famous contribution to the psychological literature is his concept of the collective unconscious. With this new formulation Jung broadened Freud's limited conception of the personal unconscious as the seat of hidden instinctual energies to include universal symbols that are shared by all humanity. These can emerge as archetypal images within an individual's psyche via dreams, art work, and fantasies. Through his concept of the collective unconscious, Jung provided a rationale for a psychological substratum that is larger than a person's limited individuality. In this sense, all humanity possesses the same "mind" and

36

each individual can draw shared contents from these depths.

Jung went even farther and developed a concept of the Self that to some extent mirrors his idea of the collective unconscious. While Jung made different uses of this term in various parts of his writing, the most relevant definition for our purposes is to designate Self as an all-embracing unitive organizing principle in the life of a person.[11] Jung made a distinction between the individual ego and the Self: the ego embodies most of what we know in the West concerning the personality (the sense of being a separate person with specific feelings, ideas, sensations, etc.); the Self subsumes, precedes, and goes beyond the ego. Just as the collective unconscious reflects a universal character which dwarfs the personal unconscious, so too the Self represents a deeper level of identity which is larger than individual human beings with all their personal hopes, fears, joys, and sadnesses. The Self is larger than one's self-concept, than individual neuroses or hang-ups, than personal character traits, and so on. Moreover, this Self (which existed even before the physical birth of the person) is larger than the growth of the individual ego as it moves through the various stages of human development charted by contemporary developmental psychology. In fact, Jung suggested that the Self is in some respects the director or orchestrator of that very process of development. This role, he asserted, could be observed most clearly during times of personality change, when the individual ego is undergoing a process of individuation and transformation. At times such as this the Self comes to the fore, helping to redirect and retrue the patterns of growth inherent within the individual.

Jung's concepts of the collective unconscious and the Self are relevant to my purposes in this book because they provide a framework for understanding some of the nonordinary childhood experiences surveyed thus far. Many of the images that surfaced in these experiences (e.g. Black Elk's visions of his ancestors, the starfish in a young girl's "big dream," the angels in Lilly's church experience, etc.)

could be interpreted as archetypal experiences that tap the contents of the collective unconscious. Moreover, it may be that the children who experience a sense of unity, light, love and a feeling of some greater presence in their lives are connecting to the Self.

Jung came to a similar conclusion after studying some of the "big dreams" of childhood. Originally Jung thought that these archetypal dreams reflected the unconscious of the children's parents and were not really coming from the children themselves. Jung frequently stated in his writings that children's lives reflect the unspoken lives of their parents.[12] At times he treated adult patients who did not dream by analyzing the dreams of their children. He felt that their children's dreams would accurately pinpoint areas of conflict present in the adults. However, eventually he came to realize that the "big dreams" of childhood are more than mere reflections of an adult unconscious, that they come from deeper centers of the child's own psyche. In fact, Jung had a "big dream" of his own when he was three or four years old, a dream which he said "was to preoccupy me all my life."

> I discovered a dark, rectangular, stone-lined hole in the ground. I had never seen it before. I ran forward curiously and peered down into it. Then I saw a stone stairway leading down. Hesitantly and fearfully, I descended. At the bottom was a doorway with a round arch, closed off by a green curtain . . . Curious to see what might be hidden behind, I pushed it aside. I saw before me in the dim light a rectangular chamber about thirty feet long . . . The floor was laid with flagstones and in the center a red carpet ran from the entrance to a low platform. On this platform stood a wonderfully rich golden throne . . . Something was standing on it which I thought at first was a tree trunk twelve to fifteen feet high and about one and a half to two feet thick. It was a huge thing, reaching almost to the ceiling. But it was of a curious composition: it was made of skin and naked flesh, and on top there was something like a rounded head with no face and no hair. On the very top of the head was a single eye, gazing motionlessly

upward . . . Above the head . . . was an aura of brightness. The thing did not move, yet I had the feeling that it might at any moment crawl off the throne like a worm and creep toward me. I was paralyzed with terror. At that moment I heard from outside and above me my mother's voice. She called out, "Yes, just look at him. That is the man-eater!" That intensified my terror still more, and I awoke sweating and scared to death. For many nights afterward I was afraid to go to sleep, because I feared I might have another dream like that."[13]

This dream is interesting because it contains elements of both the earth (subterranean cavern, fleshy phallus) and spirit (the eye of the phallus and the bright light above it). Thus it seems to embody both lines of development suggested in this book ("up from the body," "down from the spirit"). Much later in his life Jung continued to ponder over this dream:

Who spoke to me then? Who talked of problems far beyond my knowledge? Who brought the Above and Below together, and laid the foundation for everything that was to fill the second half of my life with stormiest passion? Who but that alien guest who came both from above and from below?[14]

Jung frequently stated in his writings that the first half of life is basically a time for ego development, a movement outward into the world with its responsibilities and commitments. In his view it is only during the second half of life that true spiritual and religious questioning and questing can begin in earnest.[15] Yet according to what we have seen in Jung's own experience, childhood can be a time, at least for some, when the basis for that inner quest is laid. Frances Wickes, a leading Jungian child psychiatrist, suggested:

Experiences of timeless realities may come to the very young child . . . As the child grows older, problems of the outer world press upon him. His ego must grow to meet the demands of greater consciousness and numinous experience may appear to be forgotten by the ego, but it is remembered by the self—that sage who from the beginning lives in the psyche of the child and speaks the defining word in times of peril.[16]

Dora Kalff, another well-known Jungian child psychotherapist, shares the story of a twelve-year-old boy who had been brought to her for therapy because of his withdrawn nature, even though by all accounts he appeared externally well adjusted to society. Using the medium of a sand tray (a miniature set of figurines and a sand box), the boy constructed a scene that depicted an enormous battalion of heavy artillery guns opposing a line of three small guns protected by flimsy tin fencing. The child was asked, "Can these three weak artillery units really withstand the heavy weapons?" The boy answered: "One never knows." Kalff went on to comment:

> I am deeply moved again and again at the discovery of how close the child's psyche is to spiritual and healing forces. The simple words of the child "one never knows" expressed at the same time a profound, worldly wisdom which reminded me of the Chinese sage, Lao-Tse . . . "That which is weak conquers that which is strong/And what is tender conquers what is tough . . ."[17]

Kalff pointed out how the three guns represented the possibility of healing in the child, the chance that his fortressed aggressions could somehow be confronted by "his apparently still-weak energies which essentially 'are bigger than our ego.' "

These dynamic energies are always there in some form above or below the surface of our externally developing ego—the ego that is observed and measured by contemporary developmental psychology. But the Self is not so easily detected by the instruments of psychology. It may only become apparent during times of crisis, or as a whisper in the midst of the louder forces of adjustment and adaptation to cultural realities. Yet the Self is ultimately an ally to the child's developing ego. When external adjustment has reached an impasse or does not reflect the deeper creative urgings of the child, the Self may rise to the fore and provide what Jung called the "compensatory function," creating a realignment in the balance of intrapsychic functions, and a healing within the child's inner being.

Psychosynthesis and the Higher Unconscious

Roberto Assagioli, the founder of psychosynthesis, was an Italian psychiatrist whose origins were in the psychoanalytic tradition of Freud. He, like Jung, broke away from Freud's teachings when it became clear that there were areas of the human psyche omitted from Freud's scheme. In particular, Assagioli was concerned that Freud's system sought to dissect the human personality without giving the patient a means of integrating what had been analyzed. Hence he created *psychosynthesis*, a system whereby that which had been taken apart could be reordered, synthesized, and integrated. Figure 1 depicts Assagioli's model of the person.

1. The Lower Unconscious
2. The Middle Unconscious
3. The Higher Unconscious or Superconscious
4. The Field of Consciousness
5. The Conscious Self or "I"
6. The Higher Self
7. The Collective Unconscious

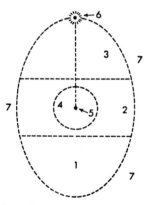

Figure 1. Assagioli's Model of Consciousness[18]

According to this model, the everyday waking state of the person is designated by Region 4 in Figure 1 with the point labeled 5 representing the sense of "I-ness" that makes up our primary experience of identity. Like Freud, Assagioli spoke of the unconscious, but he made some important distinctions between levels of the unconscious which are crucial in our understanding of non-ordinary childhood

The Radiant Child

experiences. What Freud designated as the unconscious or subconscious, Assagioli regarded as the "lower unconscious" (Region 1). According to Assagioli, this is the seat of basic drives, instincts and urges, complexes, psychological correlates of physiological functions, lower uncontrolled parapsychological processes, and various phobias, obsessions, and compulsions. In addition, in his model Assagioli included the collective unconscious (Region 7), which Jung spoke of, and also the middle and higher unconscious. The middle unconscious (Region 2) represents a part of the psyche that is near to waking consciousness and easily accessible to our conscious life. It contains many automatic functions that we do every day without realizing how we do them (like driving a car), and also serves to incubate ideas and images before they emerge into full consciousness. The higher unconscious (Region 3) according to Assagioli is the place where "we receive our higher intuitions and inspirations—artistic, philosophical, or scientific, ethical 'imperatives' and urges to humanitarian and heroic action. It is the source of the higher feelings, such as altruistic love; of genius and of the states of contemplation, illumination and ecstasy. In this realm are latent the higher psychic functions and spiritual energies."[19]

Assagioli's model allows us to make some general distinctions between different kinds of non-ordinary experiences. As quoted above, Assagioli notes that the lower unconscious includes "lower uncontrolled parapsychological processes." This would probably include the clairvoyant abilities of Peterson's students, many telepathic abilities in childhood, and poltergeist phenomena. It does not, however, include the intuitive insights, wisdom, deep religious, "peak," or archetypal experiences surveyed in Chapter 2. These latter forms of non-ordinary experience fit better with the "higher unconscious" or even "the higher self" in Assagioli's model (shown in the diagram as a dotted line extending from 5 to 6).[20]

Assagioli did not create a developmental model based on

this concept of personality, nor did he concern himself much with childhood. However he did have an interest in the capacities of gifted children and saw the potential for spiritual awakening within them.

> Super-gifted children show at a very early age an interest in philosophical, moral, and spiritual subjects. They often possess real intuition and spiritual illumination.[21]

The possibility that even "normal" children may be able to demonstrate this same interest has been explored by psychosynthesis educators Paula Klimek and Jack Canfield. They conducted a project entitled "The Radiant Student." Canfield and Klimek led a group of eleven- and twelve-year-old children through a series of psychosynthesis exercises designed to help them get in touch with deeper levels of inner knowing. The focus of the work was a full-length body tracing which students carefully embellished with symbols and designs reflecting their discoveries from the exercises. Canfield reported:

> The results were phenomenal. Many students drew in the chakras, pineal glands, auras, healing energies emanating from their hands, archetypes, symbols, and on and on. There had been no previous discussions of any of these concepts. What emerged was spontaneous and magnificent.[22]

One of the exercises that Klimek and Canfield used was called the "Life Purpose Fantasy." Children were instructed during relaxation to review their entire lives in reverse. When they had reached the moment just before birth, it was suggested that they experience meeting a special guide or wise person who would be able to help them answer the question, "What is the purpose of my life?" Some of the children's responses were:

> I walked through a meadow with lots and lots of flowers, and at the end there was a colored spiral pattern . . . I met a woman and she gave me . . . a red rose. She had really deep purple eyes that kept me in a sort of trance. The quality was a sort of inner warmth or beauty.

> I started going down a rainbow. I rode with all the kids
> I ever knew, and all around I saw things that have hap-
> pened to me in the past. I also saw the word "love" all
> around me.
>
> I saw a path through the woods all over the world. I had
> endless limits of what could happen.[23]

The exercises employed in these experiments appeared to
establish a connection between the limited individuality
of these children and something larger and more comprehensive.

Welwood and the "Open Ground"

John Welwood, a transpersonal psychologist, provided a
very different interpretation of the unconscious from those
of Jung and Assagioli. Rather than regarding the unconscious as a "realm" or "place" (e.g. "collective unconscious,"
"higher unconscious," "lower unconscious," etc.) distinct
from conscious experience, Welwood sought to convey the
idea that unconscious processes operate as "fields" of awareness that interact in flexible and dynamic ways with conscious processes of focalized awareness. In fact, Welwood
pointed out that attention itself (what we would call "consciousness") is always shifting from relatively discrete levels
of awareness (as for example when we hear a loud sound) to
progressively more diffuse or "fuzzier" patterns of awareness. Welwood calls each of these fields a "ground" (the
background component of the figure/ground dichotomy).
He enumerated four kinds of "ground" that represent progressively more diffused and comprehensive patterns of
awareness:

1. *The Situational Ground.* Sometimes referred to as "felt
meaning," this level of awareness describes the implicit or
prearticulate feelings we have concerning our ever-changing lived situation. Welwood illustrates:

"If you the reader stop and think for a moment of some
person you know, you may notice that behind any specific

thoughts, emotions, or images you may have about the person, there is a whole fuzzy 'feel' which is quite different from the felt sense that you may have for any other person."[24]

2. *The Personal Ground.* Welwood defines this level as "the way in which personal meanings and associations, developed during the individual's life history, presently shape consciousness in a background way."[25] This level can include a whole range of memories, fantasies, projections, likes and dislikes, and feelings that we are usually not aware of unless through meditation, therapy, or introspection we focus awareness on them.

3. *The Transpersonal Ground.* This level represents stepping back even farther into a more generalized background of awareness. It is against this backdrop that we sense "the wisdom of our organism," the over-all directing energies implicit both within the cosmos and within ourselves as individual personalities. It includes the larger sense we have of our own interrelatedness to all living things, of our place within the biosphere. It is our sense of "being-here," both as a separate person and as a universal embodiment of living principles within nature.

4. *The Open Ground.* This most diffuse level of awareness, also referred to as "open space," is "pure, immediate presence before it becomes differentiated into any form of subject-object duality."[26] Called by Buddhists "primordial awareness" or "no-mind," this is the ultimate background of consciousness, without form or content. According to Welwood, this basic open ground can break through into normal consciousness as fleeting glimpses or flashes during meditation, in the space between sleep and waking, or even in the course of our everyday activities. This ground is generally crowded out, however, by all the other interpenetrating grounds and by our normal focalized attention that always seeks to fill in awareness with names, labels, concepts, and feelings.

Welwood has suggested that children in particular are more sensitive to the "open ground" than most adults:

It seems that children, especially before the consolidation of their sense of personal identity, live closer to open space than adults in many ways. They change quite rapidly, incorporate all kinds of contradictions, and do not need a consistent *persona* to refer everything back to. They have frequent "lapses" into what appears to be "empty-mindedness," which might be called "spacing-in." The child's spacing in is different from distracted "spacing out" . . . in that the child is still naturally close to an open ground, which gradually becomes more and more obstructed as he gets older.[27]

The "open-ground" experience may be what is going on in some of the unitive or peak experiences reviewed in Chapter 2, although it seems likely that more of them were related to the "transpersonal ground," especially where a sense of the "inter-relatedness to all living things" is concerned ("in that moment I knew that I had my own special place, as had all other things . . . "). Still other experiences—especially the psychic ones—may be part of the "personal ground," reflecting a melange of emotionally fused images that are partly projection and perhaps partly a tapping into the personal grounds of other people.

Ken Wilber and the Spectrum of Consciousness

In the past ten years Ken Wilber has emerged from a quiet obscurity to become one of the premier theorists in transpersonal psychology. He has written a series of remarkably synthetic books which apply his theories to a wide range of fields, including developmental psychology (*Atman Project*), anthropology (*Up from Eden*), the sociology of religion (*A Sociable God*), and psychotherapy (*No Boundaries*).

Wilber has utilized a "spectrum" approach to viewing psychological development. Just as white light contains a range of frequencies or levels of vibration, so too can the panorama of consciousness be broken down into a spectrum of levels. Figure 2 summarizes Wilber's characterization of these levels with respect to individual human development.

Wilber has called this developmental progression "the

Atman project." By this he means to describe the process by which Atman (Ultimate Reality) projects itself onto the

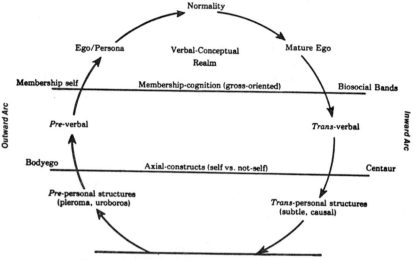

Figure 2. Wilber's Levels of Consciousness[28]

screen of the illusory world (the Outward Arc) and then begins to pull itself in to discover its real identity as the Absolute (the Inward Arc).

The individual begins development at levels which Wilber terms "pleromatic" and "uroboric". These are "pre-personal" structures reminiscent of our earlier discussion of the material and unconscious beginnings of the child in a state of fusion with the mother. Out of this pre-personal unity, children begin to establish a rudimentary sense of self rooted in the physical body (body-ego). They then move toward an internalization of cultural rules and patterns of interaction within the family (membership self) on the way to developing a stable and fully functioning ego at the height of the Outward Arc.

The second half of the developmental cycle, the Inward Arc, describes those levels that are beyond our notion of the average adult in society. They include the "mature ego," in which adults have developed as much as possible within the limited confines of their culture. In other words, one with a mature ego has learned all the rules of the game, as it were, and now begins to go beyond the "biosocial bands" or meta-rules which bind societies together.

The transverbal levels of development are populated by the artists, philosophers, writers, and other geniuses of a society who have gone beyond levels of "normality" in an effort to transform the structures of the culture. The centaur level describes the full flowering of the individual personality. It is to the "trans-personal" levels that the individual now turns in a process of giving up a sense of separateness and identifying with progressively deeper and broader aspects of the Self. The transpersonal realms describe the experiences of saints, mahatmas, avatars, and other mystics of the East and West. The journey culminates in identification with the ultimate as Atman or Pure Being.

Wilber's model provides a way of describing and relating stages of growth from the most primitive levels of unconsciousness to the most superconscious levels of transpersonal awakening. His model unifies a broad range of psychologies, including traditional Western developmental models (Piaget, Freud, Erikson, Mahler, Baldwin, Sullivan, etc.) in the pre-personal and egoic levels; humanistic and existential psychologies (May, Laing, Rogers, etc.) in the mature egoic and trans-verbal levels, and Western and Eastern mystical traditions (Vedanta, Tibetan Buddhism, mystic Christianity, etc.) in the trans-personal levels.

Childhood is generally relegated to "pre-personal" and early egoic levels in Wilber's developmental scheme. Wilber himself has frequently stressed the importance of not confusing the "pre-personal" unitive experience of the infant or child with the "trans-personal" experience of the mystic (a mistake Wilber called a "pre-trans" fallacy). A full discussion of this question is reserved for Chapter 7. For the present, suffice it to say that while some of the psychic experiences surveyed earlier seem to belong to the prepersonal stage of development, many other experiences do not and appear instead to be situated at the other end of Wilber's spectrum (subtle, causal, and ultimate realms). Although I might seem to be guilty of committing the pre-trans fallacy in saying this, actually I am drawing upon one of Wilber's own concepts—the emergent-unconscious—in making sense of these higher experiences in childhood. One of five types of unconscious processes described by Wilber, the emergent-unconscious, contains all those levels of development yet to unfold within the individual.[29] Hence, if an individual is at the ego/persona stage of development, the emergent-unconscious would contain all subsequent levels, including the mature ego, centaur, and all transpersonal structures (subtle, causal, and ultimate). Wilber has suggested that an individual at a given stage of development may experience the emergent-unconscious as the breaking through into awareness of the next-higher level. For example, an individual at the centaur level might begin to experience foreshadowings of the subtle level.

Wilber does not seem to allow for the possibility of experiencing levels far beyond one's present stage. Yet it would seem that this is exactly what has occurred in many of the unitive experiences described in Chapter 2. Children who are in many other ways identified with pre-personal or early egoic levels of development seem to contact, if only briefly, those levels of consciousness on the far end of Wilber's developmental continuum.

This does not seem unusual if one understands that these levels *are already present* within the child's psyche in latent form, as Wilber has aptly noted: "We can begin by agreeing with Vedanta that *all* levels and stages are one with Self."[30] Hence, although a child usually proceeds stage by stage through the various levels of Wilber's hierarchy ("up from the body"), many of the "spirit down" experiences cited earlier seem to represent a departure from this orderly process. Wilber may be referring to this when he observed that "the subtle [level] can begin to emerge . . . usually after adolescence, but rarely before."[31] How rare these experiences actually are remains to be seen. Yet it seems clear that they do exist, and that their existence signals a broad departure from the majority of Western developmental psychologies.

Unanswered Questions

While the four models presented above appear to be useful in making some general distinctions among major groups of non-ordinary experience (e.g. psychic vs. spiritual), there are still many "grey areas" where multiple interpretations are possible and the exact nature of a given experience is unclear. For example, we do not know whether Chamberlain's hypnotically regressed subjects were operating from a pre-personal parapsychological symbiosis (based on psychological unity with the mother) or were connecting instead with their "higher selves." We do not know if Black Elk's childhood illness precipitated a delirium which activated archetypal images from the collective unconscious or whether he managed to break through into a "transpersonal ground" of awareness.[32] The near-death experiences surveyed in Chapter 2 are equally puzzling. In some respects they seem to have clairvoyant characteristics related to Assagioli's "lower unconscious" (visions of dead relatives, tunnels, etc.). Yet they also seem to tap aspects of the "higher unconscious" insofar as they brought with them a deep sense of happiness or peace. Clearly the lights which Peterson's school children so matter-of-factly described came from a psychological level different from the healing light of Yogananda or the meditation light of The Mother. Yet the celestial lights of the near-death experience are not so easily plotted on a map of the psyche.

The models which have been presented here should be seen as general guides that are useful in clarifying non-ordinary experiences but hardly a substitute for the experiences themselves. Ultimately, each experience of non-ordinary reality is unique in itself and must be considered on its own merits. It seems entirely possible that many of the experiences thus far explored are multifaceted events that draw upon a variety of levels and require a whole range of psychological maps and research tools in order to be properly understood. Hopefully, the child psychologist of the future will be fully trained and equipped to deal with such a panorama of experiences.

4

The Child as Exile: The Mythological Approach

The story of Adam's exile from the Garden of Eden shows that there is a certain time in a man's life when he is in the Garden of Eden, and after that time he is exiled from there and no longer experiences that joy and happiness and freedom that once the soul possessed. There is not one soul in this world who has not experienced the Garden of Eden, and that Garden of Eden is babyhood.[1]

Hazrat Inayat Khan

An extraterrestrial being is stranded on planet Earth after being accidentally left behind during a secret reconnaissance mission from another planet. A small boy finds this stranger, and together they plan a way for the alien to get back home. This simple scenario outlines the basic plot of the movie *E.T.: The Extra-Terrestrial*, one of the biggest box-office attractions of all time. At least part of the fascination felt by so many people with the film *E.T.* seems to stem from the fact that children (and many adults) strongly identify with E.T.—a being who is in exile, stranded in an alien world, and searching for a way to get back "home."

This theme of exile is not a new one. Its roots are buried deeply in ancient mythology. One version of the exile theme—and the one that will concern us in this book about childhood—has come to be known as "the infant exile motif." This theme has occurred and recurred in thousands of myths in widely differing cultures and historical epochs. When it appears, one can be certain that the mysteries of human origins are being explored. The infant exile theme serves as an allegory for the life of any infant. In some respects, it is *the* myth of human development, charting out the course of the hero-ego from its divine origins to its noble destiny. This chapter will explore the infant exile motif and related mythological themes, in an attempt to discover how certain non-ordinary states of early childhood may be related to memories of a lost paradise or kingdom from which the soul has been exiled.

Otto Rank, one of the early figures in the psychoanalytic movement, summarized the basic structure of the infant exile motif in his description of the myths surrounding the births of mythological heroes and religious figures. Although many of the details of the motif vary across cultures and traditions, Rank has expressed most of the basic elements of the motif in the following description:

> The hero [to be exiled] is the child of most distinguished parents, usually the son of a king. His origin is preceded by difficulties, such as continence, or prolonged barrenness, or secret intercourse of the parents due to external prohibition or obstacles. During or before the pregnancy, there is a prophecy, in the form of a dream or oracle, cautioning against his birth, and usually threatening danger to the father (or his representative). As a rule, he is surrendered to the water, in a box. He is then saved by animals, or by lowly people (shepherds) and is suckled by a female animal or by an humble woman. After he has grown up, he finds his distinguished parents, in a highly versatile fashion. He takes his revenge on his father, on the one hand, and is acknowledged on the other. Finally, he achieves rank and honors.[2]

Rank distilled these common elements of the motif from an analysis of over seventy different stories in mythology and religion concerning the birth of the hero. The figures whose life stories fit at least part of this basic pattern include: Sargon, Moses, Abraham, Oedipus, Judas, Paris, Krishna, Perseus, Gilgamesh, Cyrus, Tristan, Romulus and Remus, Hercules, Jesus, Buddha, Zoroaster, Siegfried, and Lohengrin. Two of these legends have been selected to further illustrate the nature of this motif: the birth and early histories of Siegfried (from Teutonic mythology) and Perseus (from Greek mythology).[3]

Siegfried

King Siegmund of Tarlungaland was upset when he was told by Count Hartvin that the king's wife Sisibe had been having illicit relations with a menial. This of course had not really happened. Count Hartvin was merely spreading lies because he had been spurned by the queen. The king, however, not knowing this, was advised to have the queen's tongue cut out. He sent Count Hartvin and Count Hermann into the forest to do this. However, the two counts started quarreling while on the way there because Count Hermann did not want to go through with the deed. While they were arguing, Sisibe gave birth to a remarkably beautiful child and placed him within a glass vessel. As the fight between the two counts came to a close, Count Hartvin, in the process of falling in defeat, accidentally kicked the vessel into the river, and it was swept downstream to the sea. The queen died in a swoon when she saw this happen.

After a time, the vessel was swept by the sea's tide onto the shore where it broke, releasing the young child, who had grown somewhat in the meantime. Hearing the child's cry, a doe picked him up and carried him to a den where he lived for twelve months. One day the child ran into the forest and was found by a childless smith named Mimir who raised him as his own son. Mimir gave him the name Siegfried. Siegfried grew to an enormous stature and attained great strength. This was too much for Mimir to bear and he sent Siegfried into the forest to be destroyed by Mimir's brother, a dragon named Regin. However, Siegfried killed both Mimir and the dragon and then proceeded to the princess Brunhilde who named his parents for him.

Perseus

Acrisius, the King of Argos, had become old and still had no son. He consulted the Delphic oracle who warned him against male descendants. The oracle said that his daughter Danae would bear a son who would rise up to kill him. Fearful for his life, Acrisius locked his daughter up in an iron tower and had it heavily guarded. Despite this precaution, Zeus penetrated the tower in the form of a golden shower and impregnated Danae. She bore a child whom she named Perseus.

One day Acrisius heard Perseus inside the tower, and he killed the nurse and took mother and child off to the altar of Zeus to have her swear an oath that Zeus was the father. Even though she did so, he did not believe it and put mother and child in a box which he threw into the sea.

After a time, the box was picked up in a net by a fisherman named Dictys, and he took Danae and the child home and lived with them as family. However, his brother Polydectes fell in love with Danae and, wishing to get rid of Perseus, sent him off on what he hoped would be a fatal mission to retrieve the head of the Gorgon Medusa. Perseus accomplished this task and many others besides.

Finally, one day while engaged in a disc-throwing competition, Perseus accidentally killed his grandfather Acrisius, thereby fulfilling the old prophecy. The young hero then took his place as king of Argos and builder of Mycenae.

Theories About the Infant Exile Motif

Several interesting theories have been proposed by psychologists to explain the almost universal presence of the infant exile motif in mythology. Both Otto Rank and Carl Jung noted that this motif occurred in the fantasies of disturbed young children (and adults), "who, believing themselves to be infinitely finer and greater than their parents, imagine that they must actually be of noble, even divine descent, but exiled or lost, and only adopted by this coarser pair [e.g. a smith, a fisherman, animals, etc.] that they have been taught to revere as parents."[4]

Otto Rank gave a classic psychoanalytic explanation for this motif. He believed that it describes the situation of children who desire that their parents remain larger than life and all-protecting, as during the early years of life "when . . . father still appeared to be the strongest and greatest man, and . . . mother seemed the dearest and most beautiful woman."[5] The psychoanalytic view stresses the need of children to let go of these unrealistic perceptions of their parents at the time of the Oedipal crisis (about five years of age) and accept their parents as fallible individuals ("the coarser pair").

R. D. Laing provided an explanation that probes more deeply into the origins of human life. He suggested that the infant exile motif is in fact a parable of the zygote's journey down the uterine canal on its way to becoming implanted in the uterus and growing from embryo to fetus to newborn baby.[6] In this analogy the zygote is the child-hero, the uterine canal is the river into which the hero is thrown, and the uterus represents the adopting function (like the rescuing fisherman in the Perseus myth). In this view the motif represents a kind of deep memory of our own biological origins.

I would like to suggest a transpersonal correlate to Laing's biological explanation.[6] In this view the infant exile motif is a deep memory of our own *spiritual* origins in Essence, Spirit, or Selfhood. The hero in this interpretation is the soul, cast out of its unity with the Self or Spirit (noble parents) and set adrift, only to reach land (become embedded in matter) and begin the long and arduous task of reclaiming its nobility (reuniting with the Self or Spirit) in adulthood.

The infant exile motif contains elements that relate to both lines of child development suggested in this book. The exile portion of the myth seems to describe the journey of the child *down from the spirit.* Many of the non-ordinary experiences described by Traherne, Wordsworth, Robinson, Yogananda and others in Chapter 2 may represent memories of "divine origins" by the exiled child-soul, memories of a time when the child was still close enough to her "native land" to catch glimpses of the timeless bliss or eternal harmony that constitute the fabric of that deeper Reality.

The second line of development is suggested in those portions of the myth that begin when land is reached. The child is found and nurtured. The child-hero then begins a series of heroic battles with monsters or rivals on the way to reclaiming his nobility in adulthood. These events appear to describe the ascent of the soul *up from the body*. At the same time, there are portions of this motif where the two lines of development seem to intersect. The rest of this chapter will explore these interweaving strands of development, both with respect to the development of the child and in terms of their reflection in mythological themes worldwide.

Memory of Spiritual Origins

Evolutionists, cultural anthropologists, sociobiologists and most contemporary scientists trace the origins of the human species back to the animal kingdom, with roots deeply embedded in biological processes. However, this is only half of the story, the half suggested by the evolutionary or "body up" line of development.[7] There is considerable evidence to suggest that a complementary view of human development would include a descent from spiritual realms as well.[8]

Helena Petrovna Blavatsky, one of the founders of the modern theosophical movement, spoke of the first living beings as "self-born . . . from the brilliant bodies of the Lords."[9] This view parallels stories of human origins in most of the world's mythologies and religions. In many of these stories humans are regarded as *descended* (in the sense of having "come down") from giants, angels, gods, and other deities, and are not necessarily or totally the progeny of the apes.

In the Judeo-Christian tradition this sense of origins is conveyed in the story of the Garden of Eden and the expulsion from Paradise.[10] In this metaphor Eden represents the original state of spiritual unity or harmony with God, with the Fall as the descent into matter (the emergence of evolutionary development, or in individual terms the beginnings of ego separateness). The Hindu tradition suggests another way of interpreting the spiritual descent of humanity. In their cyclical view of time the Hindus divide history into four major epochs or "yugas" that repeat themselves continually. One such cycle or "maha yuga" takes 4,320,000 human years or 12,000 god years to be completed. The first age, or the Krita Yuga, is the "golden age," when spiritual understanding is at its height. The succeeding ages begin the process of deterioration in values and morality until the fourth or "Kali Yuga," our present age, has been reached. At these times materialism and selfishness are at their maximum, only to be succeeded by spiritual renewal and the beginning of the new Maha Yuga or cycle of time.[11] In this scheme one can look back not to only one golden age, but to countless golden ages in the past, and also to countless golden ages in the future.

The Hindu view is corroborated in other mythologies. The Greek tradition speaks of four races—golden, silver, bronze, and iron—which succeed one another in descending order. People of the golden race lived like gods, free from pain, toil, and old age. In the silver race childhood lasted a hundred years. Those of the bronze race by contrast became increasingly war-like until, with the advent of the iron race, destructiveness was paramount.[12] This same perspective is reflected in Persian mythology, where Zoroaster was said to have seen a vision of a tree with four branches, gold, silver, copper and iron, and was told by Ahura Mazda (God) that there were to be four kingdoms of Iran, each worse than the previous.[13]

Humanity's search for lost worlds points to an awareness that there was at one time a golden age. Ever since the time of Plato, there have been rumors of a utopian world that existed in the far-distant past—beyond the reach of historians—when life was in many ways more advanced than our present civilization. The search for Atlantis, Lemuria, Shambhala, and a host of other forgotten civilizations has been colorful, though often riddled with hoaxes, charlatanry, and wishful thinking.[14] However, a few researchers have been successful in demonstrating that these worlds may have actually existed.[15] What is more important, an incredible *search* has gone on for hundreds and even thousands of years in an attempt to find these lost lands. Such a quest suggests an intense longing for a golden time in the past when life was more harmonious than it is today.

Many hold that these lost worlds are not to be found in archaeological digs or in secret mountain hideaways, but deep within the human psyche. The description that Edwin Bernbaum, a student of Tibetan culture, gives in his book *The Way to Shambhala* sounds as much like a spiritual journey into the depths of the soul as it does a physical trek to the Himalayas. As Bernbaum points out:

> Myths of hidden places like Shambhala help to remind us, if only subconsciously, that there is much more to the world than we imagine. Without something to inspire a sense of the unknown, of a realm beyond conception, our lives become closed and static, limited by the superficial views we hold. Rather than being just a form of escape, our interest in Shambhala actually reflects a deep longing to experience reality itself. We might say that the kingdom represents the place in each of our lives where we make contact with the world in which we really live.[16]

Bernbaum continues by relating this experience of the unknown to the experiences of childhood:

> When this awareness appears, it brings back the forgotten memories of childhood experience. It reminds us of a time when we did not know what the world was like, when everything seemed as unknown and mysterious as Shambhala. At that age we had no preconceptions to cover up and dull our perceptions. Rather than fitting things into fixed ideas of how they should be, we experienced them directly, with all the sense of awe and wonder they inspire. As a result, the world around us had the fresh and magical quality of a hidden kingdom.[17]

Yet, as we have seen, even children sense themselves not as residents of Paradise but as exiles cast out of the golden land and forced to persevere in a strange world. The plight of the child is much like the complaint of the exiles in *Psalm 137* who sat by the streams of Babylon and wondered aloud: "What, should we sing the Lord's Song in a strange land?" Using this biblical reference as a departure point for speaking about the child, Clifford John Williams, a Quaker artist, suggested:

> For a child the land is even more "strange" than it is for us. He grows up in a family and a house that he has not chosen and does not possess, and he is subjected to a series of rules and arrangements about which he is not consulted; he is indulged sometimes, caressed and played with, while at other times he is told to run along and not be a nuisance. He is injected, dosed, fed, and dressed according to the prevailing fashions in these things, and packed off to school to obey another set of rules and punishments about which he has not been consulted. He is told that some things are right and some things are wrong, but is rarely told why these things are so or whether they have been and will always be so.[18]

A Stranger in a Strange Land: The Hero Quest

As distasteful as this exile is for the child, it is a real and an inevitable fact of life. The glass vessel travels across the ocean and shatters against the rocks, leaving the young child defenseless against the elements. Fortunately, the forces of nature are often kind, and "animals or humble folk" come to rescue and help the child grow to maturity. Yet the child still has many battles ahead. It is this phase of the child's existence that characterizes development "up from the body." Mythologically, this line of development has been described by individuals such as Joseph Campbell in his *Hero with a Thousand Faces* and Erich Neumann in *The Origins and History of Consciousness*. In a more psychological vein, it has also been described by ego psychologists, cognitive psychologists, and others concerned with the stages of development that a child goes through on the road to maturity.

Neumann's description of this phase of development is most appropriate here because of his rich use of mythological terminology in relationship to the growing child. According to Neumann, a Jungian psychoanalyst, the child begins life symbolically embedded in the uroboros. This ancient symbol is frequently represented by the image of a snake swallowing its own tail. By this image Neumann suggests the child's total unity with the mother, a unity so complete that there is no sense of mother or of a separate self. From this original state, the child must emerge as an individual. The emerging ego-self, Neumann suggests, is the figure represented in all cultures and traditions as the hero.

The hero must encounter many inner and outer forces (tasks, labors, difficulties, demons, adversaries) as he seeks the light of consciousness or "the treasure hard to attain" (a symbol of integration or spiritual attainment). Initially the child must come to terms with the awesome image of The Great Mother. She represents materiality or nature and is a force of sustenance and nourishment, but she also seeks to drag the hero back into a state of dependency and unconsciousness.[19] Perseus' decapitation of the Gorgon Medusa represents a triumph of the hero over a particularly negative version of the mother archetype. Out of the image of The Great Mother, other forces emerge which must also be "slain" (integrated with the psyche).[20] One such image is that of the dragon, which is often a representation of one's own unconscious instinctual life. Siegfried's victory over the dragon Regin signifies an important step in his battle for freedom from the cloying bonds of the unconscious.

The quest of the hero, then, parallels the development of the child. Having come from nobility to a lowly residence, the child must now win back his noble heritage through brave deeds and adventures. As Bernbaum notes:

> Most people never go beyond this stage; they remain caught in the conflicts of the surface consciousness, unable to get what they want or to see themselves as they are. If, after many years of struggle, a person manages to overcome his illusions and permanently awaken the deeper mind, he recovers the fresh vision of a child, enriched and deepened by the wisdom of experience."[21]

Help from Above

During the quest to develop ego-structures and attain maturity, the child-hero often stands alone. Yet mythology sometimes shows a figure appearing and providing a source of assistance, often at a moment of seeming defeat.

Jungians would say this figure comes from a deep level of the psyche. Many times, help comes from earthy sources (an animal, a gnome, a fisherman). This form of aid could be said to represent support and nourishment of the child's growing ego as it seeks to become strong enough to meet the forces of the outside world. At other times, however, this help is more transpersonal in nature and serves to remind the hero of his essential divine or noble identity. In Tolkien's *Lord of the Rings*, help came in the form of Galadriel's gift of a vial of light to Frodo, which he took with him into the darkness of Mordor. In Greek mythology, it was the thread that Ariadne gave to Theseus which brought him safely through the dangers of the labyrinth. It might have been that very same thread which in George MacDonald's *The Princess and the Goblin* helped the princess find her way back to her great-great-grandmother from the dark recesses of the underground land of the "cobs."

Joseph Campbell comments on the significance of the helper in myth and legend:

> What such a figure represents is the benign, protecting power of destiny. The fantasy is a reassurance—a promise that the peace of Paradise, which was known first within the mother womb, is not to be lost; that it supports the present and stands in the future as well as in the past (is omega as well as alpha); that though omnipotence may seem to be endangered by the threshold passages and life awakenings, protective power is always and ever present within the sanctuary of the heart and even immanent within, or just behind, the unfamiliar features of the world. One has only to know and trust, and the ageless guardians will appear.[22]

Helper images can represent "spirit down" forces that assist the ego-hero with "body up" tasks, challenges, obstacles, and responsibilities. These forces (angels, ancestors, guardians, etc.) are embodiments of a divine presence which exists within the psyche from the very beginning.

These energies remind us of who we really are. Often they come at times when we seem most hopelessly embedded in ignorance/materiality, and then they prod us on to further efforts in regaining our spiritual birthright. Many of the experiences of light, wonderment, harmony, and integration in childhood cited in Chapter 2, might be interpreted as helpers of this kind.

The effect of such timely reminders is often far-reaching and deeply felt throughout the course of a lifetime. Sometimes they come in the form of a dream.

> Such a dream came to a three-year-old child and lived on in the psyche of an old, old woman until it blossomed into a faith by which, in her old age, she lived; a faith in life itself, to which she sought to give testimony. She did not tell the dream; she knew that her life must be a revelation of its truth if she would give testimony to its reality, if it were to live . . . . All the details are forgotten. Only the final picture remains clear. "I am in a high meadow, unknown yet strangely familiar. In its center is Behemoth: huge, terrifying, evil. By his side, unafraid and rooted in its own serenity, is a single bluet, that smallest flower of meadow or woodland, tiny, fragile in its four-petaled innocence . . ." To the child become an old, old woman who still held the dream in remembrance, it became a symbol of the faith by which she lived.[23]

Thus it is that the child as exile is not entirely alone in her journey through life. Accompanying her in the great adventure is a picture of her own origins in perfection, a blueprint of spiritual essence that is both beginning and end. This picture forms the larger pattern within which the smaller personality navigates and serves to assist the ego in finding its way back to the source of all things.

5

The Child as Soul: The Metaphysical Approach

In Mira's family a young girl of two or three years sang a tune and was saying to herself, 'It is the tune I sang when I was a shepherdess in Greece.' The memory of it was evoked at such an early age possibly by her fine psychic nature. It is not latent or precocious genius here, but memory.[1]

Sri Aurobindo

As a very young child, Ratana Wongsombat accompanied her step-grandfather to the Wat Mahathat (Buddhist place of worship) in Bangkok, Thailand. She demonstrated a familiarity with the surroundings, in the monastery, although she had never been there before. She asked for money to give to the beggars and before giving it to them, folded her palms in salute. Without being told, she went to buy flowers, candles, and incense sticks at a nearby stall. Then, when the adults who accompanied her wished to go into the temple, Ratana told them that they must first worship the Buddha's relics and directed them to another building. At this location, she knelt down in the manner of an adult, placed a handkerchief on the floor, and put the flowers on it. Later during the ceremony in the main temple, Ratana was observed murmuring silently while the others chanted. A nearby woman asked her how many of the Buddha's precepts (vows) she wanted to keep. Ratana replied, "five precepts." When asked how many precepts her father kept, Ratana replied: "probably eight." Her replies were consistent with the Buddhist doctrine of five elementary precepts plus three additional precepts for more advanced practitioners. Ratana had been told none of this previous to her visit to the wat.

After returning from the wat that night, her stepgrandfather asked her—perhaps humorously or perhaps in sheer amazement at her precocity in the temple that afternoon —where she had been before this life. Ratana said, "Which part should I tell you?" She then related that in a previous life she had lived in a green hut, had meditated there, had been driven from the hut and moved to a nearby district in Bangkok where she eventually became ill, had an operation, and died.[2]

The case of Ratana Wongsombat is one of over 2000 "cases of the reincarnation type" which Dr. Ian Stevenson, a University of Virginia psychiatrist, has collected over the past twenty years. The case of Ratana Wongsombat was an exceptional one for her precociousness. Dr. Stevenson related:

> A typical case of this type begins when a small child, usually between the ages of 2 and 4, starts to tell his parents, and anyone who will listen, that he remembers living another life before his birth . . . . A child claiming to remember a previous life usually asks to be taken to the place where he says he lived during that life . . . If the child has furnished enough details . . . the search for the family of the person he has been talking about is nearly always successful . . . . The child is then usually found to have been accurate in about 90 percent of the statements he has been making about the deceased person whose life he claims to remember.[3]

Dr. Stevenson's own meticulous investigations of these cases are included in several academic journals and five books.[4] He has been careful to rule out other possibilities such as family collusion, mental telepathy, and other potential causes of these phenomena. He points out that such cases do not *prove* the validity of reincarnation but rather strongly suggest it. In any case, his research and the data generated from it are unparalleled in contemporary psychiatry and deserve careful study.

Stevenson's findings, if true, could revolutionize the way we view children in the future. His research suggests that children are more than tiny personalities in the act of unfolding, but rather that they have brought with them into this lifetime a rich storehouse of experience built upon the efforts of previous lifetimes. This new perspective of childhood would regard the child not as a small ego, but as a soul; a being whose essential nature remains the same underneath or above the surface of an ever-changing series of life histories. The structure of the soul and its relationship to the personality have historically been the province of religion and philosophy. It is to such a "metaphysical" interpretation of childhood that we now turn.

The Levels of Selfhood

In the West since the time of Descartes, we have been conditioned to think of the person as consisting primarily of a physical body that is the source of all secondary processes such as perceptions, feelings, and thoughts. If we are religious, we may entertain vague thoughts about a soul or spirit existing in some way as well. However, the ruling scientific paradigm of the Western world does not admit to a soul since it regards the physical body as the generator of all possible forms of consciousness and behavior. In this model of reality, once the physical body is gone, we are gone. Here, the person is reduced to the firing of neurons and the flowing of hormones.

It has not always been this way in Western thought, nor is this scientific/reductionistic viewpoint shared by much of the world. Among the ancients and even in the Middle Ages, the concepts of soul and spirit were well-known components of the human being and were applied as rigorously to the study of the person's inner nature as today's concepts of neurotransmitters and action potentials are applied to the workings of the human brain. Huston Smith, noted authority on comparative religion, has spoken of these ancient "levels of selfhood" as being fourfold: *body, mind, soul, spirit.*[5] These levels are still an important part of many esoteric and metaphysical teachings.

In this conception of selfhood, the body is simply the most dense layer of the self, and the terrestrial world exists as a condensation or crystallization of more subtle and rarefied forms of being. Our physical bodies are the outermost level; that aspect of being which functions like an overcoat. It is the first part of the person to be seen and also the first part to be discarded. This version of reality essentially stands materialism on its head by regarding the body and physical matter as the *outcome* and not the *source* of all experience.

The mind (seen here to consist of perceptual, emotional, and mental elements) exists as an entity in its own right. While the materialistic bias of rational Western thought regards the mind as a function of the physical brain, this older model of selfhood sees the mind as existing independently of the brain.

Just as the mind exists apart from yet appears to integrate and unify the physical structures of the brain, so too the soul could be said to exercise a synthesizing effect on the structures of the mind. In this model the soul is more than a poetic image. It represents a viable ontological entity that according to Huston Smith is "the final locus of our individuality."[6] The soul is the bridge between ourselves as separate human beings and a universal background of oneness. We may think of ourselves as being some *thing* in particular (a body, a great intellect, a passionate individual) and identify with many different sensations, feelings, ideas, and roles. Yet the soul exists both within and also beyond the flow of these inner worlds that we have built for ourselves. It observes, reflects upon, permeates, yet stays apart from the din of our daily lives. That is why the ancients regarded the soul as the part of ourselves which continues to exist after the death of the physical body. They described the capacity of the soul to transcend body and mind and affirmed its ability to soar off to other worlds and experiences—perhaps to other lifetimes as well.

The spirit represents the universal aspect of ourselves; our ultimate identity with the life of the Cosmos. The soul is the core of our individuality, while the spirit is the ground of *all* individual lives and is beyond all lives as well. It is Life itself, infinite, transcendent, yet immanent within everything that exists.

This conception of human nature has been stated in one form or another for thousands of years. With roots in antiquity, it has found expression through many different religious traditions and esoteric philosophies, including yoga psychology, Vedanta, Sufism, Gnosticism, abhidharma Buddhism, and Kabbalistic studies. More recently one version of this fundamental view was presented by H. P. Blavatsky, who reintroduced "theosophy" (theo: God; sophia: Wisdom) to Western readers with her seminal book *The Secret Doctrine* at the end of the nineteenth century. In that work Blavatsky combined the wisdom of ancient and contemporary schools to support her explorations of the essential being of the Self. Since that time many students and teachers have restated and interpreted various aspects of the theosophical world view.

One essential feature of theosophy involves a further elaboration of the fourfold levels of selfhood in the model presented above. This theosophical model is sometimes characterized as having seven levels or "fields" that are progressively more refined and comprehensive in nature, with each field interpenetrating all others. These include physical, etheric, emotional, lower or concrete mental, higher or abstract mental, intuitional, and spiritual. The first two fields correspond to *body*, the second two to *mind*, the third two to *soul*, and the final to *spirit*. In addition, the first four are sometimes referred to as the *personality*.

The Physical Vehicle

This, the most obvious level of the self, reflects the structure of the physical world and leads to the identification of self with a corporeal body, our densest mode of being. The experiences of the physical world include sensations resulting from external stimulation (the perceptions of the five senses), as well as sensations emerging from within the body itself. Though it is structurally the "lowest" or outermost aspect of self, all other levels, including the highest spiritual realms, interpenetrate this grossest of forms. While an exclusive identification with this "food-body" (Sanskrit: *annamayakosha*) will shut out awareness of higher spiritual values, many traditions including yoga and tantra have sought to utilize the physical body as a medium through which the spirit can be realized.

The Etheric Field

Sometimes called the "vital body," this level is generally considered to be part of the physical realm. One might say that it consists of the most rarefied forms of physical matter, subtler even than gases. Generally, this field is invisible to the average person, but certain individuals (including many children and also trained clairvoyants) are reported to have a capacity for perceiving this field as an emanation of energy around the physical body. This is sometimes referred to as the "aura" of the person (although the aura can include other fields as well). Spiritual traditions have termed this energy field prana (Hindu) or chi (Taoism). The etheric level is described to a certain extent by "morphogenetic fields," theorized by plant physiologist Rupert Sheldrake.[7] Like an M-field, the etheric field provides the matrix within which life structures (e.g. a physical body) can develop. Although it may seem that the etheric emanates from the physical, it is in fact the other way around. The physical is essentially enfolded in and permeated by the etheric and receives its sustenance and its vitality from this subtler realm. Sometimes called the "etheric double," this level is also referred to as the "health body" of the individual because, according to clairvoyants, frequently the source of disease appears in the etheric form of the person long before it manifests as a physical illness.

There have been many recent efforts both to measure this energy field and to make use of its energies to help promote well-being. Parapsychologists have developed techniques such as Kirlian photography and the use of dicyanin screens to record the presence or absence of energies at this level. Holistic health practitioners with some knowledge of etheric energy flow in the body have developed new methods of healing such as Therapeutic Touch, which incorporates the ancient ritual of the "laying on of hands."[8] Acupuncture may also be working at this etheric level.

There is an easy way to get a general sense of this field of energy. Find a partner and spend some time in a relaxed posture with your palms uplifted and held a few inches from your partner's palms. With eyes half closed, see if you can sense an energy field between your hands and your partner's. Move your hands back and forth slowly until the sense of a ball of energy or a pulling sensation is felt. This feeling may be an experience of etheric energy.

The Emotional Field

This level is the source of passions, drives, moods, images, and impulses, an ever-changing, kaleidoscopic field of emotional states in a continual state of transformation. Experience here ranges from emotionally laden sensations and perceptions that are close to the physical level to passionate impulses that soar up to spiritual realms. This is the field that reflects continually evolving desires. Clothed in the garb of imagination, these emotional responses essentially create entire inner landscapes for an individual. Contemporary Western psychological traditions have mapped out part of this realm and called it the unconscious.

However, the emotional field, sometimes called the *astral* realm, extends far beyond individualistic notions of a personal unconscious. Like all the superphysical fields, it consists of a continuum that extends throughout all space. Our individual emotional fields are localizations in this universal field, much as the field around a bar magnet is a localization of the magnetic field that exists everywhere as a potential. The astral field all around us is said to include a whole fauna and flora of superphysical beings such as angels, fairies, and entities passing between lifetimes.[9] In addition, it serves as the repository for a range of crystallized mental energies, sometimes called "thought forms," that are the product of individual and collective ideas and desires.[10] One might equate this realm, at least in part, with Jung's collective unconscious, although it permeates our conscious lives as well, and, according to theosophy, exists independently of human consciousness.

To get a feeling for the emotional or astral field, pay attention to your dream life. The contents of your dreams, especially when they are clear or "lucid" dreams, will give you a sense of the quality of the astral. On an interpersonal level, think about a time when you met a new person and something didn't feel "quite right" in the new relationship, or alternatively where you felt an immediate attraction to someone. You may have been responding unconsciously to the emotional field of that person. Or you may get a special "feel" in certain environments, depending on the quality of astral energy that permeates them. Consider for example the different kinds of "vibes" that are experienced in a haunted house, a cottage in the woods, a seedy bar, or a stately cathedral.

The Lower or Concrete Mental Field

This level embodies various aspects of intellectual functioning. On the lower levels of this field, the intellect serves to organize various sense impressions into perceptions of the objective world, the so-called "sense-mind" (*manomaya-kosha*). At this level the intellect is also closely tied to the emotions, so that thoughts can be colored by a desire for gain, a fear of loss, and the motivation to come out ahead of others in a competitive grab for pleasure and possession, as well as sympathy and the desire to help others. The concrete mind also helps us organize our daily lives and assists in handling practical matters.

The mind at this level is the source of our categorizing things into pigeonholes. It tends to divide and separate, perceiving the world as made up of discrete entities. This tendency is the source of our seeing ourselves as separate beings, cut off from everything and everyone around us. As such, the concrete mind represents the "flowering" of the Western rational mind, with both its powers and its limitations. With its full development, we come to the completion of the sphere of the personality as measured and studied by traditional developmental psychology. Beyond these "lower vehicles" (physical, etheric, emotional, and concrete mental) there are "higher vehicles" which are the province of esoteric schools, spiritual traditions, and transpersonal psychologies.

The Higher or Abstract Mental Field

As we move up the vibratory scale of mental functioning, the intellect becomes progressively more clear, objective, and free of egotistical bias. It begins to perceive a broader and more selfless view of life as it ascends through levels of scientific interest and artistic pursuit to philosophic realms where creative interconnections and synthesis are paramount. Ultimately, it reaches up toward high levels of illumination and insight which border on true spiritual understanding and intuition. The abstract mental field is the realm of the "witness" or "observing self" which views the goings-on of the "lower selves" with detachment and compassion. It is said that this realm contains the memory imprints of past lifetimes.

We have all caught glimpses of a higher level of mental functioning when contemplating a problem. During the early stages of the problem, the mind is cluttered with ideas that compete for attention and have a "confused feel" about them (the realm of the lower concrete mind). Then at some point in this process (frequently after a time of rest or incubation), the mental field suddenly undergoes a radical reorganization, much as a pile of iron filings on a metal plate move into geometric patterns when a magnet is held under them. Suddenly we experience a sense of "Aha!" and achieve a deeper insight concerning our problem. We may experience new relationships and connections or synthesize radically disparate elements in achieving a creative solution. This "Eureka!" phenomenon offers a hint of what the creative and organizing effect of the mental field is like when we undergo a spontaneous transformation and reach its level.

The Intuitional Level

This realm, which is referred to as *buddhi* in Vedanta philosophy, has been characterized as a "bliss-body" (*anandamayakosha*) that experiences beatific visions, transcendent levels of illumination, and a deep sense of oneness with all life. This is the sphere to which many saints and mystics have ascended in their meditations, becoming conscious of a panoramic spiritual world beyond words and rational explanations.

As it permeates the lower levels of the self, the intuitional field is perceived more as what we commonly call intuition and a sense of the presence of higher worlds. As I. K. Taimni points out:

> When the vibrations of the Buddhic plane are . . . stepped down into the physical brain, they lose much of their intensity and appear in physical consciousness greatly toned down by transmission through the intermediate planes. Thus the direct perception of the unity of Life on the Buddhic Plane becomes merely an all-embracing compassion and sympathy, direct insight into Truth becomes merely intuition and knowledge of the truths of the higher life.[11]

We may perceive this field of being in flashes of inner truth, perhaps during a time of quiet contemplation or during moments of intense creative activity. This may be the realm of Maslow's "peak experience" and could be the source of many of the transpersonal experiences reported in this book.

The Spirit

This component of self is more than a level or field. It essentially represents the core of our being. If termed a field, then it would be the ultimate ground of being spoken of by Paul Tillich, or the "open ground" of the Buddhist psychologist John Welwood. It is the source of all of the other vehicles or fields. According to some traditions, it is the only true representation of Self, all other fields, levels, and bodies being merely reflections of this essential core. In its individual aspect, it has been called Atma. In its universal aspect it has been referred to as Paramatma. Many traditions have other names and descriptions for this level of being: God, Absolute Reality, Christ Consciousness, Clear Light, Sunyata, Turiya, the Void, Brahman, the Beloved. While traditions differ in the way they characterize this level, all are in agreement that it is the essence of Self, whether it be of fullness or emptiness, and only through it do all other fields have their existence.

It is important to keep in mind that the seven levels or fields of consciousness just described are *not* heaped on top of each other like a stack of dominoes. Rather, each level interpenetrates every other level; the highest is in the lowest and vice versa. In reality, there is only one indivisible wholeness, one primal cosmic energy that animates all life and is none other than Life itself. Yet this energy *appears* different as it enlivens different levels and is dimly observed or experienced by an individual caught in the web of ignorance.

In essence, then, these seven levels or fields represent seven layers of increasing clarity with regard to Ultimate Reality, though they all express some facet of that Reality. The varying levels play themselves out in a person through the chakras (Sanskrit for "wheels"). These are built-in energy vortexes that exist on different levels and mediate between the many different fields of consciousness, helping to integrate or unify them all within a human life.

Metaphysics and Child Development

Now that we have briefly explored some basic metaphysical conceptions of selfhood, we can proceed to apply these principles to our understanding of non-ordinary experiences in childhood. First, it seems clear that traditional Western psychologies have restricted their studies of the child to the development of *personality* or the lower vehicles or fields of selfhood. Within their own domain, what they have described is in many ways consistent with esoteric psychology's description of how the personality unfolds. Figure 3 adapted from Rudolph Steiner, presents a summary of the stage-by-stage evolution of personality from the perspective of esoteric psychology.

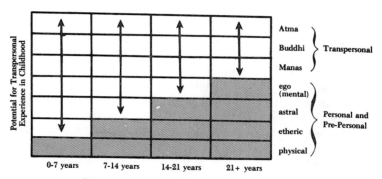

Figure 3. Steiner's stages (adapted)[12]

Both esoteric and traditional psychology agree that the child begins personality development primarily as a physical organism. Freud spoke of the child's instinctual nature during the first five or six years, and this approximates the seven years ascribed by esoteric psychology to the development of the physical field.

Esoteric author Rudolph Steiner asserts that a major transition takes place at around age seven with the change of teeth. He claimed that this event signals the release of energies centered around the etheric field and ushers in a whole new realm of thought for the child.[13] This comes close to Piaget's observations that around the age of six there is a change in the child's ability to think, a transition from "egocentric" and "paradoxical" thinking to what he called "concrete operational thought." Steiner holds that there is a release of hitherto dormant astral or emotional energies at adolescence. This agrees with the findings of psychology and psychiatry concerning the tremendous emotional changes that accompany puberty.

Finally, Steiner perceived complete mental functioning (development of the ego or concrete mental field) as occurring at about age twenty-one. This oversteps the traditional psychological assignment of the highest forms of cognition to early adolescence (Piaget's stage of formal operations occurs between the ages of eleven and fourteen). However, if one thinks of mental functioning in the terms described in the section on the concrete mental field, then it is possible that these mental capabilities in their many forms may not become fully developed until the beginning of adulthood. Our Western society has traditionally viewed twenty-one as the ripening of one's ability to function in the adult world, and this agrees in principle with the esoteric view of the completion of personality.

Esoteric psychology parts company with traditional developmental psychology primarily with respect to the higher fields of selfhood (which are not even recognized by mainstream Western psychology). The esoteric conception sees the development of personality as occurring within a broader context. The child is more than the growing body, the developing emotional life or the evolving intellect. The child as personality is enfolded within a larger whole represented in general by the soul and spirit, or more specifically, by the higher fields of selfhood (abstract mental, intuitional, and spiritual).

Since in this view children are souls as well as personalities, they have access to higher fields even while their lower fields are unfolding. This potential is suggested in Figure 3 by the arrows at each stage of development. These arrows illustrate the possiblity of the spirit or soul, through the higher fields, making contact with and interpenetrating the lower fields of personality. Speculation below, based on the previous description of the levels of selfhood, suggests how non-ordinary experiences fit within these esoteric models.

Non-ordinary States at the Personality Level

Many of the psychic experiences described earlier, including clairvoyant visions, mental telepathy, and poltergeist phenomena, could be regarded as coming from the etheric and/or emotional fields. According to esoteric psychology, the child, especially before the age of seven, is exceedingly sensitive to the contents of the etheric and emotional worlds. Laurence and Phoebe Bendit, a psychiatrist husband and psychic wife, suggested: " . . . in terms of etheric anatomy, [the child's] psychic-centers—the chakras—are open and unprotected, like the windows of a house before the glass is put in.[14] This means that anything that happens to be in the psychic environment of children can enter their etheric field, whether it be the thoughts of others, archetypal configurations from the unconscious of the parents, or any of a host of paranormal entities or energy forms. As accurately pointed out by Piaget, Freud, and others, the child at this age cannot distinguish between what is external and what is internal, between what is "fantasy" and what is "reality." According to the esoteric perspective, part of the difficulty is that many forms of psychic phenomena appear to be as real to children or even *more real* than commonly observed events in the objective universe.

As children move toward school age, they receive stronger messages from adults and peers that non-ordinary kinds of experiences are incompatible with what is emerging as the "official" version of reality. In consequence, these experiences are repressed, forgotten, or simply kept to one's self. This process of withdrawal from psychic sensitivity finds a corresponding development in the child's psychic anatomy. The Bendits base the following description of the child's etheric field on clairvoyant observations:

> Usually around seven, the chakras change. At birth they are to be seen as shallow depressions on the surface of the aura, with a thin channel like a stalk running back to the etheric spinal cord. Gradually, however, they deepen, and at the same time come forward beyond the surface of the etheric so that they are like cornucopias or nasturtium flowers growing from the spine, and they develop a fine mesh of etheric energies like a membrane, over the open end. This membrane or web has a special function, in that it filters the impacts from the psychic world and limits what enters physical consciousness. In this way it not only shuts out invasion from the objective physical world but also from the personal unconscious or subjective psychic world of the individual himself.[15]

As a result of this filtering process, the psychic senses tend to close down after the age of seven in most children, and nonordinary experiences of this personality-bound kind become less frequent.

Paranormal experiences can recur, however, at the time of adolescence, when the emotional (astral) field is being integrated into the personality. This process can disrupt the emotional balance between the different chakras or energy centers that had been achieved in middle childhood. Changes at adolescence can also disturb the "etheric web" and allow psychic material once again to flow into conscious awareness. This suggests why poltergeist phenomena (associated with the astral plane) occur generally in situations where an adolescent is present. It also helps to explain the fascination so many teenagers have with the supernatural, the occult, and the demonic (all aspects of the emotional/astral world).

Non-ordinary States at the Higher Mental Level

The higher or abstract mental field is said to contain memory traces or impressions (*sanskaras*) that are held by the soul, and not by the mind as we understand it in the West. This view implies that the soul is capable of identifying with successive personalities and carrying experiences from one personality to the next. This process, of course, is commonly referred to as reincarnation. Although the concept of reincarnation is thought to be held by only a few exotic religions, it is closer to the truth to say that it has been entertained in one form or another by virtually all the world's major religions and has been a powerful guiding force in the histories of many civilizations. In addition, it has guided the lives of many creative individuals, including Pythagoras, Plato, Caesar, Ovid, Dante, Spenser, Milton, Voltaire, Goethe, Emerson, Churchill, and Joyce.[16]

There are many versions of what occurs when the soul reincarnates. The theosophical version has it that at the time of physical death, the soul disidentifies with the physical body and lingers for a time in the realm of the emotional (astral) and lower mental fields. During this time it experiences a range of positive and negative phenomena, the sum total of which determine whether that experience is one of "heaven" or "hell." Unlike the Christian conception of these worlds, esoteric philosophy holds that heaven and hell are not eternal and objective regions but are temporary states of one's own creation. After experiencing these self-made realms, the soul continues onward to higher mental levels, where it experiences a long period of rest, reflection, and relaxation. Once this period is over, the soul begins the journey back into a physical body, a descent that is propelled and structured by the karmic propensities of the soul (the need to experience the fruits of actions from past lifetimes).

An alternative version of this process is given by Tibetan Buddhism: At the time of physical death, there is an experience of the Clear Light of Absolute Reality, which is essentially a reflection of one's own true nature. If one does not immediately identify with this Clear Light, there is a second opportunity to achieve union with another lesser Clear Light. If this second opportunity is not seized, there is a progressive movement "downward" through many diverse phenomenal realms, some heavenly and some hellish, which can lead to various forms of rebirth. Finally, the soul is blown by the "winds of karma" into another physical body.[17]

Children are still close to the portals of the birth experience and thus may possess vivid memories of what transpired during a previous incarnation. Since they are more than personalities in the metaphysical view, one could say that their soul retains the memories of these past lives. This is suggested by the work of Ian Stevenson. The children in his studies seem to have gained access to their own higher mental fields within which are encoded the events and experiences associated with a previous existence in a different personality structure.

Non-ordinary Experience at the Intuitional Level

The intuitional field was described as the realm of bliss, ecstasy, spiritual illumination, and divine insight. As such it could be the level accessed by those children whose peak experiences were described earlier. This might be the level reached by Jean Houston in her "moving into meaning" at the age of six, or by the young boy who had a sense of being "ancient" at age seven, as reported in Chapter 2. Here, the intuitional realm seemed to manifest as a flash of insight rather than a sustained state of consciousness. Hence these experiences may have been "stepped-down" versions of "the real thing" experienced by advanced spiritual practitioners.

Paradise and the Planes of Consciousness

A child's encounter with the higher fields of awareness charted in esoteric philosophy may parallel the mythological themes explored in Chapter 4. Memories of a lost paradise could be nothing less than the dim awareness of a time when the soul was passing between lifetimes and glimpsed the Clear Light of Reality of the Tibetan after-death state, encountered "heavenly" states of ecstasy on higher mental planes, or remembered times of spiritual attainment from past lifetimes. The "noble parentage" of the infant exile motif may be a reference to any or all of these states.

Yet, as noted earlier, the child must be exiled from these paradises. It is the price that is paid for taking an incarnation in a physical body. Yet there are rewards to be found in such a courageous descent. The physical world serves as a proving ground for the ecstasies that were so easily attainable on the higher planes between lifetimes. The real task of life, according to many spiritual disciplines, is to bring down that higher knowing into the grossest and most unknowing levels of (un)consciousness. This is what makes the child's experience of timeless realms so important. If children are able to catch a glimpse of those worlds and hold on to a picture of that experience as they move through adult life with all its tasks, responsibilities, challenges, and obstacles, then this higher reality can be nurtured like a seed in winter, only to be transformed in time into the most beautiful of spiritual blossoms.

6

The Child as Healer

Grown men may learn from very little children for the hearts of little children are pure, and, therefore, the Great Spirit may show to them many things which older people miss.[1]

Black Elk

Recently I was at a conference held at a picturesque seaside convention center. I was having lunch in the dining hall and was discussing with a friend some of the morning's workshops when one of the dining hall administrators passed by my table hurriedly and spoke brusquely to a coworker as she passed: "I don't care! If they come in late, they'll just have to leave when we tell them to!" Clearly, the woman was harried from the afternoon rush. I returned to my lunch and forgot about the incident until perhaps half an hour later when my attention was turned toward a scene that took place a few yards from my table. A mother was carrying her young infant and there beside her, talking in loving and adoring tones to the little baby, was the same woman who minutes earlier had seemed so boorish. There was something about that infant that allowed the woman to unfold, to relax, to unguard herself from the stresses of her job and open up to an entirely lovable and loving personality.

Was the infant a healer in this case? Although the example seems rather trivial in itself, it represents, I feel, something deeper about the capacity of the child to heal, to transform, to point the way. This chapter will explore the potential that children have as healers in our culture. As I proceed with the discussion, I will use the word *healing* in the broadest possible sense. Implied within this notion of healing is the idea that something that has been wrong is being made right. This sense of healing can apply to our common conceptions of physical healing, but it can extend beyond this to emotional and spiritual healing and guidance. It can involve the healing of an individual, an entire community, or humanity itself. Living as we do in an era where, as Yeats pointed out, "things fall apart," the child stands as a symbol of regeneration, of the healing of social wounds and collective hurts, as well as of the transformation of the individual psyche.

The idea that children may function as healers in society appears initially untenable. Children seem to be the *least* likely of any in society to provide a healing function, since they lack the know-how, skills, and experience necessary to accomplish physical, emotional, or spiritual healing. Moreover, children are themselves defenseless, vulnerable to the onslaught of viruses, accidents, psychic traumas, and other malevolent events. It is *they* who are most in need of assistance from the adult healers of the culture. They need help in building up immunities to disease, in acquiring the skills and competencies necessary to avoid accidents, and in achieving the psychic defenses that will protect them against emotional trauma.

This view of children needing help is accurate from a "body up" perspective. However, there is a complementary view to childhood and healing that I would like to present. It is based on a "spirit down" view of development in which the child is seen as a metaphor for the very act of healing. Because it is a metaphor, this perspective cannot always be applied literally to the actual processes of healing. I am not going to attempt to glorify children by claiming that they can cure physical and emotional illness in the ways that a medical doctor or a psychotherapist can cure them. Yet I do claim that children have access to healing energies not available to the average adult and that this makes them qualified to discharge certain healing functions appropriate to their particular developmental level. By presenting a perspective on children as healers, I intend not only to expand our conceptions of childhood but also to enrich our understanding of the healing process at any age.

The Child as an Archetype of Healing

In his thought-provoking essay "The Psychology of the Child Archetype," Carl Jung presented a twofold picture of the universal child which parallels the "body up"-"spirit down" dichotomy. He saw the child as infantile *and* divine, vulnerable *and* indestructible, immature *and* wise:

> The "child" is all that is abandoned and exposed and at the same time divinely powerful; the insignificant dubious beginning, and the triumphal end. The "eternal child" in man is an indescribable experience, an incongruity, a handicap, and a divine prerogative; an imponderable that determines the ultimate worth or worthlessness of a personality.[2]

The child archetype forms an integral part of the human psyche containing within it the potentials for both disease (abandonment, exposure, vulnerability) and healing (divinity, regeneration, new beginnings). The healing function of children is well documented in world mythology. Asclepius, the legendary Greek physician who was later deified as god of the healing arts, is generally portrayed in iconography as a child, a youth, or an elder.[3] Apollo, the Greek patron of physicians and healing (and the father of Asclepius), founded his Delphic shrine while still a child. Apollo performed mighty feats at Delphi while still a child, including the destruction of a primeval monster.[4] We have already seen in Chapter 4 how countless other child heroes from mythology overcame their exile and abandonment in the face of seemingly insurmountable odds. These children had a divine connection with healing and nurturing energies, both in nature (help from animals and simple folk) and the heavens (help from the gods). While the destiny of many of these child-heroes did not come to fruition until their mature adulthood, still as children they fought and won many battles, which testifies once again to the healing and regenerative capacities inherent within the childhood state.

The Child's Openness to Healing Energies

It is a commonly accepted fact in folk wisdom that children heal quickly. They often become ill with astonishing suddenness and just as suddenly become well again. This is frequently observed in children with fevers: a child may develop a sudden temperature of 103° and a few hours later be back to normal. As George Meek points out in his book *Healers and the Healing Process:*

> Often the most dramatic results of healing occur with children and animal pets. They know only that there is something wrong and they want to get better. Children have yet to build a belief system based on the idea that most healing comes from pills, injections, prescriptions, or adjustments.[5]

In the theosophical world view surveyed in Chapter 5, this phenomenon of quick healing in children can in part be attributed to the child's sensitivity to subtle life energies of the "etheric field." As we have seen, young children have an innate sensitivity to this level of energy (especially before the age of seven) and fall prey to its malevolent elements as well as deriving sustenance from the healing qualities embedded within it. Mythologically, these elements have been portrayed as living entities: devils, angels, evil kings, or animals, some helping to promote disease, others serving to nurture health. Psychologically, they have been portrayed as constructive and destructive thoughts. From the metaphysical perspective, Phoebe and Laurence Bendit have pointed out how the young child is open to the "psychic atmosphere" of the etheric field, especially within the matrix of the family. If the father is constantly angry, for example, his destructive thought forms can penetrate the child's etheric field and later manifest as physical illness,[6] even though the anger may not be directed at the child. Likewise, if mother meditates on spiritual principles (even while bearing the child in the womb), these elevated thought forms can manifest as healing energies and protect the child, even from the father's anger.[7]

Developmental Stages of Healing

As already pointed out, children are not healers in the sense that we understand the doctor, the psychiatrist, the shaman, or the body-worker to be healers. However, children have their own role as healers within the community, and their function varies according to their developmental level. I have worked out a scheme that describes the healing capacities of children within three broad developmental stages, each consisting of a seven-year period.

Age 0-7:   Children as channels of healing
            within the collective unconscious
Age 7-14:   Children as carriers of society's beliefs
            about healing
Age 14-21:   Children as apprentice healers

Age 0-7: Children as Channels of Healing Within the Collective Unconscious

In this model before the age of seven children seem to function as universal and unconscious healers. Rather than healing from *intention*, their ability tends to manifest naturally and invisibly in the midst of life's more obvious events. Also, rather than specific or localized healing (of a particular illness or part of the body), the healing at this level seems to occur more often within the deep structures of the community or within deep levels of the individual psyche. In the Eskimo cultures studied by Joan Halifax, healing by children was seen to occur in subtle and unseen ways:

> . . . he [Sila, a deity] has another means of (communication) by sunlight and calm of the sea, and little children innocently at play, themselves understanding nothing. Children hear a soft and gentle voice, almost like that of a woman. It comes to them in a mysterious way, but so gently that they are not afraid, they only hear that some danger threatens. And the children mention it (casually) when they come home, and it is then the business of the (shaman) to take such measures as shall guard against the danger.[8]

In this example, the children serve almost as "assistants" to the shaman, informally and unconsciously participating in the healing processes of the tribe through their subterranean communications with nature. It is as if these children were tapping into the collective unconscious and making use of that information for the healing of their people.

Another example of a child's function at the level of unconscious healing is seen in the religious conversion experience of St. Augustine:

> While in a garden, he heard a child's voice from over the wall saying "tolle lege, tolle lege." ["Take up and read, take up and read."] Seizing a copy of the Epistles of Paul which he had been reading, he opened it at random at the passage in Romans which says: "Let us walk honestly as in the day; not in rioting and drunkenness, not in chambering and wantonness, not in strife and envying." The suddenness of the voice, the appropriateness of the message—both these facts impressed themselves forcibly on Augustine's mind. He felt that it was surely a divine oracle. His doubts were resolved.[9]

The child in this example did not intend to provoke Augustine into a conversion experience. Yet the child's voice served as a vehicle for the saint to go within and discover those truths that were to change his life. He then made these insights available to his culture through his well-known

Confessions and other writings. In this sense, the child's function was both individual and universal; individual in the sense of helping to transform Augustine as a person, and universal insofar as the event itself affected the lives of millions of Christians touched by Augustine's visions and teachings.

A final example of this kind of healing potential within young children can be seen in a custom of the Huichol Indians of Mexico. At the end of the tribal year, a large fire is built. The youngest child of the tribe, who has been designated as a potential shaman-to-be, is selected to keep the fire continually fed with wood and to remain on watch for seventy-two straight hours without sleep or food.[10] The child in this ceremony functions as a symbol of the community, a manifestation of the immanence of spirit within the tribe, attending to the flame of the new year and the beginnings of new life.

Age 7-14: Children as Carriers of Society's Beliefs About Healing

Around the age of seven the child enters into society as a functioning member. It is at this time that the belief systems of the culture most strongly interface with the child's own sense of what is possible. Although previous to this time children had been receptive to their surroundings on an unconscious level, after age seven (approximately) they actively incorporate the beliefs of parents, school, and peers into their own mode of reality; the child is essentially building that model of reality through interaction with the underlying belief systems of the culture. The culture defines for the child what is possible. With respect to healing, it is the culture that defines those factors which promote and retard wellness. Usually the belief system of the significant adults in a child's life (especially the parents) provides the basis for the child's own beliefs about sickness and health. If the parents attribute healing to pills and injections, then the child is likely to place the power for healing in those things. However, if the parents embrace another version of reality, even a transpersonal vision, the child is likely to be powerfully influenced by that belief system.

Joseph Chilton Pearce presents a compelling example of the influence of belief systems on the child in his book *Magical Child.* He relates an anecdote that illustrates the power of a shared belief between father and son concerning physical healing:

> A man came to a magical child seminar as the result of an experience that had unnerved him and threatened his academic and rational world view. His eight-year-old son was whittling with a knife, slipped and severed the arteries of his left wrist. Following an instant's panic at the sight of the spurting blood, the father, as if in a dream, seized his screaming son's face, looked into his eyes, and commanded, "Son, let's stop that blood." The screaming stopped, the boy beamed back, said "okay," and together they stared at the gushing blood and shouted, "Blood you stop that." And the blood stopped. In a short time, the wound healed. . . [11]

The transmission of belief systems from parent to child is still largely unconscious for the child of this age. However, there are cultural vehicles for transmitting specific information concerning healing methods that are consciously passed on from generation to generation. Cross-cultural instances can be provided that detail methods used by elders to instruct children in the use of charms, incantations, herbs, and other healing devices and techniques. One researcher has suggested that many children's toys of antiquity were actually protective charms and prophylactics against evil influences.[12] A woman from rural Serbia recounts her childhood training in the use of healing charms: "Baba told me 'Go sit in the corner, child, and pay attention!' So I did. Later she told me what the whispering and mumbling meant. She taught me, so I learned it and remembered it and that's how I know how to say it."[13] While taking a course in cross-cultural healing at John F. Kennedy University in California, I heard class members share memories of how their parents and grandparents taught them massage techniques so that they could later massage their tired relatives! One Japanese woman recalled that some of the methods her mother showed her resemble acupressure techniques that she was now learning in her training as a masseuse.

This developmental stage deserves careful study by educators and parents, for the messages that are given to children at this age, consciously and unconsciously, can have a profound effect on their attitudes toward healing and will continue to influence them for the rest of their lives. My parents were immersed in an orthodox Western medical model (my father, a pediatrician; my mother, a surgical nurse). Hence I was raised in a life context that placed a priority on complex interventions and procedures as a means of physical healing. I remember sitting at the dinner table as a child while my parents rambled on at length about diseases with long and frightening names. One of the consequences of having grown up within this belief system is that I have constantly battled a tendency toward hypochondria; fear of illness has stricken me at times when I was most vulnerable and open to the potentials for both healing and sickness. My energy has been drawn more toward morbidity and dependency on external health practitioners for assurance than upon a sense of self-sufficiency of the powers of self-healing, and the natural tendency of the organism to move in the direction of health. My growing edge as an adult is to re-create within my being an inner belief system that affirms these latter principles of wellness.

Age 14-21: Children as Apprentice Healers

After the onset of puberty, the adolescent is now in a position to begin the actual training process of becoming a healer in the formal sense of the word. At this time some children regain psychic abilities or other potentials which have lain dormant during the previous "latency" period. It is also a time in some cultures when severe psychic crisis precipitates the inner transformation of the shaman-to-be:

> The shaman is a person (either male or female) who in
> early adolescence underwent a severe psychological crisis,
> such as today would be called a psychosis. Normally, the
> child's apprehensive family sends for an elder shaman to
> bring the youngster out of it, and by appropriate meas-
> ures, songs, and exercises, this experienced practitioner
> succeeds.[14]

Frequently in cases of this kind, the adolescent is taken by
the shaman to a remote region of the countryside where he
must endure isolation, starvation, cold, and other forms of
deprivation, often for long periods of time. In the course of
these sufferings, the youngster sometimes has a vision of a
"guardian spirit" (often in the form of an animal) that serves
as a guiding principle or "healing factor" in his future role
as a shaman. The youngster then joins the shaman and over
a period of years is taught the outward rituals and the inward principles of healing and transformation. As an adult,
he can then share these with the community in a conscious
and controlled way.

Children as Agents of Cultural Transformation

Lyall Watson, author of *Lifetide: The Biology of Consciousness* relates a story concerning the eating habits of a group of
monkeys on a Japanese island. It seems that the monkeys
were confronted with a dilemma: they enjoyed a new kind
of sweet potato that had been introduced to the island, but
balked at eating them freshly dug out of the ground and
covered with grit. One day a young monkey washed potatoes in the sea before eating them. This practice quickly
spread throughout the island as monkeys taught each other
this new method of food preparation. The story continues
that monkeys throughout the nearby islands went on eating
unwashed sweet potatoes for a time. Then suddenly, with
no physical contact with the potato washers, some of them
began washing too. It is conjectured that when the "hundredth monkey" on the original island learned to wash

potatoes before eating them, he completed a "critical mass" of monkeys that somehow influenced monkeys all across the islands so that they began using this technique in cleaning their food.[15] This "hundredth monkey" phenomenon has been used as a metaphor for what can happen when enough individuals mobilize their energies, thoughts, and actions in the same direction (for example to help promote world peace).[16]

What is particularly fascinating about this story is that the originator of this new method of washing potatoes was an *infant*, an eighteen-month-old monkey named Imo. This fact is significant because it points to the role children have in the transformation of culture. The playfulness and flexibility of childhood contributes to a state of consciousness where novel solutions and new ways of being and doing are encouraged.[17]

One of the areas in which this is most apparent is language. Kornei Chukovsky, a noted Russian children's writer, regarded the child from two to five as a "linguistic genius" capable of generating metaphors that enrich and enliven the spoken language.[18] Lewis Thomas called children "the sixth modern wonder of the world" because of their capacity to invent language.[19] He noted a phenomenon observed on the Hawaiian islands where children of workers immigrating from regions across the globe were essentially fashioning a new language from the pidgin dialect that was being used by the adults to communicate with each other. Derek Bickerton, writing in the *Scientific American* about this curiosity, noted that their new language exhibited "the complexity, nuance, and expressive power universally found in the more established languages of the world."[20]

A related example can be seen in the "music-making children" of northern Ghana. These children gather in the village squares to dance and sing, using simple musical instruments. Originally their dances and songs were re-enactments of established village music. Gradually, however, the children evolved a new dance style called Atikatika, which employs a chorus of political satire and witticisms created without any adult assistance. Because of the volatile nature of some of their songs, these dances have been frequently banned by the adults in the community, although other villagers encourage the dances. Many young people gather at the Atikatika group practices waiting to see what new things the children will do next. As one villager related, "If you want to see our way of life, you will see it from the children . . . it is the children who make our culture, because the children can do something and it will come to stand as something for the old people."[21]

Children have helped to create civilization in an even more profound way than suggested above. There are, of course, the child prodigies who contribute to society before their adulthood: Wolfgang Mozart, Blaise Pascal, John Stuart Mill, among many others. On another level, however, if we look at the lives of some of the great thinkers who transformed the way we think and live, we can see that the seeds of their inventions and ideas began in their childhood. Albert Einstein, for example, was four or five when he was given a magnetic compass that filled him with a sense of mystery and a desire to ferret out answers to the secrets of the universe.[22] Jacob Moreno, the creator of psychodrama, one of the most original and dynamic of the current psychotherapies, marked the beginning of his career from a simple childhood incident:

> Moreno historically locates the beginnings of psychodrama as occurring when he was four and one-half years old. He was playing with some friends in the basement of his house in Vienna, the city in which he spent most of his formative years, and he suggested that they all play God and angels. There was a large table in the center of the room on which were stacked a number of chairs. Moreno climbed to the very top and he played God and had the other children go around the table flapping their arms as if they were wings, taking the roles of angels. As the children assumed the roles of angels and thought of themselves as flying, one suggested that Moreno, perched high atop the chairs, fly too, and he attempted to do so. He quickly fell and broke his arm, but was left with a sense of exhiliration and spon-

taneity of the experience. Both elements—spontaneity and exhiliration—were to become central concepts in the later development of Moreno's theory.[23]

In his autobiography Leonardo Da Vinci shares the story of how a giant bird came to him as he lay in his crib. Leonardo noted that this event was connected in a significant way with his later fascination with birds in flight. Eric Neumann, the Jungian theorist, even suggests that Leonardo incorporated this early childhood experience into his art work.[24] The paintings of other great artists such as Chagall, Picasso, and Miro reveal a preponderance of child-like images. In addition, innumerable writers have derived much of their material from their early childhood experience. Witness for example Proust's *Remembrances of Things Past* and Joyce's *Portrait of the Artist as a Young Man.*

Childhood is in a sense the ground from which *all* creative work emerges. It has been suggested that the artist or scientific genius is actually someone who has managed to retain his child-like wonder and curiosity while developing the adult skills necessary to translate and adapt this innocence to the needs of the culture. J. Robert Oppenheimer, one of the fathers of nuclear energy, once remarked that "there are children playing in the streets who could solve some of my top problems in physics, because they have modes of sensory perception that I lost long ago."[25] Whether or not we agree with Oppenheimer's rather startling remark, it certainly must be admitted that childhood contains within it intangible qualities that are valuable to society.

Ashley Montagu, a noted anthropologist, builds a very solid case for the cultural importance of childhood in his book *Growing Young.*[26] In this remarkable work, Montagu described the idea of *neotony,* or the tendency of a species to retain youthful characteristics into adulthood. Montagu suggests that as species evolve there is a trend for youthful characteristics to be retained into adulthood for longer and longer periods of time. One example he uses concerns the fact that an infant ape's jaw looks more like a human jaw than that of an adult ape. Montagu extrapolates from anatomical and physiological findings such as this to psychological principles. He suggests that it is advantageous to the perpetuation of our species that child-like qualities be retained for longer periods of time, far into adulthood if possible. He noted that the physical features of the young of any species call forth from us feelings of compassion, caring, and nurturance. He also observes how childhood is a time of wonder, awe, love, playfulness, imagination, and curiosity. Montagu's research suggests that if we are to survive as a species (without blowing ourselves off the planet), then these qualities *must* be incorporated into adult levels of society.

This perspective contradicts the current and extremely popular psychodynamic world view that regards holding on to the qualities of childhood as regressive and immature. One ego psychologist has coined the term "Peter Pan Syndrome" to describe "men who have never grown up."[27] These men are described as selfish, irresponsible, unrealistic, and unfocused. Another therapist advertises workshops to help cure the "Eternal Child" of these kinds of traits. Even Jungians have disparaged the "puer aeternus" (eternal youth) of the culture who refuses to take responsibility for his life.[28] Each of these perspectives seems to have failed to understand the total meaning of childhood. Just as two lines of development in the child can be delineated, one rooted in the material the other in the spiritual, in the same way two general categories of child-ness can be described: the *childish* nature (selfish, jealous, clinging, aggressive, irresponsible, unrealistic—an "up from the body" attitude) and the *child-like* nature (innocent, wise, compassionate, full of wonder, creative—a "down from the spirit" stance). While therapists go about their job of reforming the Peter Pans of the world and curing them of their child-ishness, it is important that they take care not to squelch the child-like qualities that are so badly needed if our planet is to survive. Unfortunately, because the childish and the childlike are often found together in the psyche, the person who is "cured" of the negative aspects of the eternal child can only complain (with the individual who had been through Freudian analysis): "They have driven out my devils, but with them they have also driven out my angel."[29]

The "Inner Child" as Healer

Childhood can represent the healing state *at any age.* Adults who suffer in body, mind, and/or spirit would do well to consider the value of "becoming as a child" to help facilitate a recovery. Increasingly, evidence is accumulating in the field of holistic health studies that suggests a strong connection between emotional well-being and physical health. Many of the diseases endemic to our culture—including cancer, stroke, and heart disease—have been linked to emotional stress. Medical intervention programs are increasingly incorporating relaxation, emotional therapy, and visualization as a means of coping with and combating disease. The natural state of the child might be taken as a model of well-being. Children possess several important abilities that are keys to effectively combating disease: the ability to relax and let nature take its course, the willingness to trust those around them who are helping them become well, hopefulness and optimism, a sense of humor, playfulness, and a keen imagination.

Many approaches to emotional healing in our culture involve some kind of regression to the child state. Psychoanalysis, for example, aims at bringing the patient back to scenes of childhood traumas via dreams and free association so that the complexes originating there can be released. Wilhelm Reich, a follower of Freud, developed his own system of psychotherapy incorporating the idea that as we grow older we accumulate layers of muscular tension in response to emotional stress. This muscular "armor," as Reich termed it, needs to be penetrated so that the deeper layers of free-flowing energies characteristic of the child can once again be experienced.[30] Arthur Janov is famous for his "primal scream" therapy in which patients are taken back to childhood emotional states and helped to re-experience the rage evoked when mommy and daddy were unavailable.[31] Another form of psychotherapy, the Quadrinity Process (formerly the Fisher-Hoffman Process) uses guided imagery as a means of regressing adults back to childhood experience. It employs an elaborate series of visualizations in which adults are asked to picture their parents in a variety of early childhood scenes (such as mommy and daddy arguing). Participants in the process are assisted in re-experiencing as deeply as possible the original feelings and images of childhood, and are then taken to a further stage where those experiences are transformed into positive feelings of unconditional love.[32] Finally, in transactional analysis, the psychopathological individual is seen as playing out inner "scripts" where the "child," the "parent," and the "adult" represent different facets of the individual that must come to terms with one another. The energy and aliveness of "the child" must be recognized and honored by the "parent" (superego) and "adult" (mature ego) in this inner drama, as a precondition for mental health.[33]

In each of the above therapies, adults are helped to feel once again the vulnerability, openness, and volatility of childhood. By returning to this childlike state, energies that had been dammed up and hidden away in adulthood—with their inevitable consequence of mental suffering—are released and allowed to gain access to the rest of the personality. Psychosynthesis, discussed earlier, posits the existence within an adult of numerous subpersonalities that need to be reintegrated into the total makeup of the person.[34] Some of these subpersonalities represent the children that we have been: the angry child, the pleasing child, the loving child, the sullen child. Many people live their lives in ignorance of the way they are still affected by the children they have been. Any therapy that helps them regain contact with their "inner children" can serve to reconnect them with parts of themselves long forgotten and assist them in making contact with buried sources of healing energy.

A wonderful example of how this took place spontaneously in the life of a well-known twentieth-century thinker is given in the story of C. G. Jung's mid-life crisis. He had just broken off his relationship with Sigmund Freud—until that time his chief mentor and friend—and was plagued with feelings of self-doubt and uncertainty. One day a dream came to him reminding him of a game he played as a ten-year-old child, in which he built little houses and castles with stones and mud. Jung took this as a message that "the small boy is still around, and possesses a creative life which I lack." So at the age of thirty-eight he began once again to play like a child, gathering stones after each noon meal, and assembling them into villages as he had done many years before. Jung wrote later that this building game initiated a stream of fantasies that served to renew his creative life and provided him with a basis from which to proceed with the next phase of his life.[35]

Finally, the child-like nature can serve as an asset in the realm of spiritual healing. Most religious systems have metaphors representing God or the Absolute in maternal or paternal form. Devotees or worshippers play the role of loving sons and daughters. This spiritual relationship replicates the early childhood relationship to some degree. The spiritual aspirant acknowledges a total dependence upon the mercies and blessing of the all-powerful, all-knowing Deity, just as the child was dependent on mother and father for the satisfaction of basic needs. While some psychologists consider this spiritual relationship a regresssion to an earlier and more primitive state of dependency, an alternative view points to the healing powers that are possible within such an arrangement.[36] In spiritual practice the adult worshipper becomes a "child" and opens up to "blessing from on high." Borrowing from transpersonal psychology, we might say that the individual has broken through the barriers of the personal self and established a healing connection with the energies of the higher Self. This kind of openness to spiritual grace, whether through prayer, meditation, invocation, or other practices, can effect fundamental transformations in the life style, personalities, habits, emotional states, and physical conditions of those who make themselves "children before God."

Projects Where Children are Healers

Most of the examples cited thus far have demonstrated the capacities of children and the "inner child" to heal or transform in informal or metaphorical ways. However, there are a few recent attempts to make the healing dimensions of childhood available to others in a more literal sense. Some efforts are being made to bring together children and the elderly to effect healing, for example by placing day-care centers within retirement homes. One such center in Mechanicsburg, Pennsylvania, has been in operation since 1978. This joint venture at first had some of the elderly residents anticipating hordes of little children running amok. However, these fears have proved to be unfounded. Experience shows that with young children around the elderly residents feel less cut off from the real world and their own families. As one senior citizen put it, "the children's voices and activities add another dimension to my life."[37] Other examples of this kind of healing arrangement include Laura Huxley's "caressing centers" and Elisabeth Kübler-Ross's E. T. (Elder-Toddler) centers.

Projects which represent attempts to channel the healing energies of childhood on a planetary level include "Children as Teachers of Peace" and "Universal Children's Gardens." Children as Teachers of Peace was initiated in 1982 through the efforts of Gerald Jampolsky, a psychiatrist, and Pat Montadon, through her organizations, seeks to bring children together for the purpose of generating answers to the problems of the world. Thus far this project has produced a book of children's poetry and drawings, a series of international tours, and a peace-prize program in which children from around the world are acknowledged for expressing their feelings about peace through writing and art. The international tour program has taken small groups of children from the United States to several countries to meet with world leaders. The children have dialogued with the late Indira Gandhi of India, Chinese Premier Zhao Ziyang, Vitaly Rubin, chairman of the Supreme Soviet of Nationalities in the Kremlin, Menachem Begin of Israel, West Germany's Chancellor Helmut Kohl, as well as leaders in Japan, Taiwan, and France.[38] The peace-prize program, administered through the Round Table Foundation, recently awarded seventeen $1000 scholarships to children from Northern Ireland, Canada, England, Egypt, Israel, Greece, and Italy.[39] The project acknowledges that children have answers to world problems and that, if world leaders would only listen and act upon their suggestions, our planet could see the beginnings of a permanent peace.

The Universal Children's Garden program was initiated in 1981 to establish "1,000 local children's gardens, with one in the capital city of every nation on earth by the year 2000."[40] Largely through informal networking, this project has managed to stimulate a wide range of creative projects involving children, gardening, ecology, and world peace. The size of the projects ranges from a "one-man planter" in Mercer Island, Washington, to an entire program designed by a state-sponsored horticultural society. Recently the United Nations has granted associative status to the Universal Children's Gardens project. The current directory of gardens lists programs in ten countries worldwide. This visionary project offers a beautiful metaphor for worldwide healing and suggests, in its pairing of children and gardens, that there exists within the child a life-giving principle that holds the key for humanity's transformation.

Conclusion

Children are healers on many levels. Through their openness to subtle energies, alternative cultural realities, and developmental shifts of awareness, they allow the process of healing to occur unimpeded by rigid principles or self-limiting belief systems. Their role in healing changes according to their own developmental level, moving from unconscious manifestations of universal healing, through shared and culturally supported healing, to actual apprenticeships as intentional focalizers of healing energy.

Children are the seeds of a new humanity in more than a metaphorical sense. Through their inventiveness, openness to experience, and sense of play, they stimulate innovation and invention that can filter into and through the more mature and rigid layers of a culture, thereby transforming and enriching its fundamental visions of life. In the larger sense, childhood represents the healing state within us all. The child embodies the processes of inner and outer change and mirrors for us the fundamental structures of transformation. In the words of C. G. Jung:

> The child is potential future . . . the "child" paves the way for a future change of personality. In the individuation process it anticipates the figure that comes from the synthesis of conscious and unconscious elements in the personality. It is therefore a symbol which unites the opposites; a mediator; *a bringer of healing;* that is, one who makes whole.[41]

7

The Pre/Trans Fallacy and the Radiant Child

The golden apples drop from the same tree, whether they be gathered by an imbecile locksmith's apprentice or a Schopenhauer.[1]

C. G. Jung, Two Essays

It should be apparent by now that there is much more to childhood than has been given to us by Piaget, Freud, Erikson, and other well-known mainstream developmental theorists. Childhood is a time of transpersonal wonders as well as infantile wishes. Yet interestingly, the field of transpersonal psychology has up until now generally regarded childhood in much the same way as have traditional developmental psychologists.

The list of transpersonal thinkers who have applied nontranspersonal significance to childhood is a long and distinguished one. William James, considered by some to have been the first transpersonal psychologist, studied religious experience in adulthood but, as noted earlier, conceived of the infant's perceptions as a "blooming, buzzing confusion."[2] Carl Jung, who as we have seen valued certain aspects of the child's encounter with the numinous, general-

102

ly saw true spiritual experience as something that occurred during the second half of life. He noted that "in the early years of life . . . at most there are islands of consciousness which are like single lamps or lighted objects in the far-flung darkness."[3] Stanislav Grof, pioneering researcher in LSD psychotherapy, regards childhood experiences that surface during regression under LSD as "to a large extent in agreement with the basic concepts of classical psychoanalysis."[4] Each of these researchers seem to have stressed the "body up" line of development in making these statements.

More recently there has been a major effort within transpersonal psychology itself to clearly disassociate childhood experience from the transpersonal domain. This effort centers around a concept developed by Ken Wilber which he calls "the pre/trans fallacy." This construct, as applied by Wilber and others, discounts the possibility of transpersonal experience in childhood. In this chapter, I will take a look at Wilber's arguments and show why they seem to be ineffective in dealing with many of the childhood experiences described in this book. As we shall see, Wilber's "pre/trans fallacy" is a useful tool in discriminating levels of experience. It fails, however, when it attempts to exclude authentically spiritual childhood experience from the realm of the transpersonal.

Ironically, Wilber's early writings contain references to childhood as a transpersonal stage of development.[5] He abandoned this view in his later writings. Responding to those who equated the child's early unitive experiences with the mother as a kind of spiritual or mystical paradise state, Wilber declared:

> The infantile fusion-state is indeed a type of "paradise," . . . but it is one of pre-personal ignorance, not transpersonal awakening. The true nature of the pre-personal, infantile fusion state did not accurately dawn on me until I ran across Piaget's description of it: "The self at this stage is [still] *material*, so to speak . . . " And *material union* is . . . the lowest possible unity of all—there is nothing metaphysically "high" about it.[6]

Based upon this premise, Wilber went on to formulate the "pre/trans fallacy."[7] He claimed many theorists made the mistake either of reducing authentic adult transpersonal experiences to infantile origins (pre/trans fallacy number one or ptf-1) or of exalting infantile experiences of pre-personal unity to transpersonal status. Ptf-1 is common in psychoanalysis, as noted for example in the earlier discussion of Freud's reducing all religious feelings to infantile regression. Wilber claims that the second form of the pre/trans fallacy (ptf-2) is common in the writings of Wordsworth, Jung, Bergson, Welwood, Norman O. Brown, and others. Wilber stressed that there is nothing remotely transpersonal about the infant's "pre-" state of material unity. He noted that the child could not possibly experience the transpersonal since "it is . . . ridiculous to speak of realizing the transpersonal until the personal has been formed."[8]

Wilber's arguments are compelling and to a certain degree accurate. He is correct in making a distinction between "pre-" and "trans-" experiences in human development. However, he erred in assigning the "pre-" state to infancy and the "trans-" state to some advanced period in later adulthood. It is important to understand that both of these levels (and everything in between) exist *all of the time* in *all* individuals, regardless of their placement on the chronological age-bound scheme of human development.

Wilber does not deny this. As we have seen in Chapter 3, his concept of the "emergent unconscious" postulates this very fact. However, he is clear to point out that these levels exist as potentials only until they are made conscious in the course of development. And this development must proceed sequentially in Wilber's view. The infant must begin at the "pre-personal" level, move through egoic levels, and then (and only then) have the opportunity of reaching transpersonal levels ("usually after adolescence but rarely before").

I agree that this represents one particular direction of development, the "body up" line referred to all through this book. However, Wilber does not seem to recognize fully the possibility of a conscious descent from spiritual realms manifesting in early childhood consciousness. Wilber *is* clear to point out in *The Atman Project* that such a descent can take place. For example, in his references to the bardos or after-death states of Tibetan Buddhism, he indicates that we all essentially experience a descent from the Clear Light in each moment of our lives.[9] However, in Wilber's view this descent results in forgetfulness of those realms or loss of consciousness of them as the psyche becomes embedded in the material world.

I, too, have pointed out how this forgetfulness occurs. The major difference seems to be *when* it occurs or the degree to which it occurs in a given individual. Wilber would argue that it occurs at birth in all individuals, while I argue that it may not. Although Wilber is willing to acknowledge the possibility of a "spirit down" line of development, he abandons this notion when he refers exclusively to "pre-personal fusion" in infancy. A more complete developmental psychology would recognize the presence, not only of this material fusion consciousness, but a genuine transpersonal union with spiritual spheres. By admitting to the possibility of both of these unities coexisting in early development, we can understand why poets and mystics have spoken about infancy so differently from developmental psychologists. In this more complete view, the "pre-" level of childhood would be the realm described by Mahler, Freud, Piaget, and later Wilber. The "trans-" level in childhood would be the realm described by Steiner, Robinson, Traherne, Wordsworth, early Wilber and many of the Jungians. These latter theorists have not committed the "pre-trans fallacy." They have been talking about a different line of experience in their descriptions of childhood.

It is sometimes argued that children can't have mystical experiences because the *real* saint or sage is able to perceive higher levels of reality on a continuous basis, in a way which is integrated with all previous levels, and frequently in such a way that it can be articulated to others. Children on the other hand, if experiencing higher states at all, do so only for brief periods of time and in ways that are frequently not integrated with the rest of their primitive personalities, and in a manner that cannot be easily communicated to others. Abraham Maslow made such a distinction between children and wise adults:

> [The child] is innocent because he is ignorant. This is very, very different from the "second innocence" or the "second naivete," as I have called it, of the wise, self-actualizing, old adult who knows the whole of the D-realm [deficiency-realm], the whole of the world, all of its vices, its contentions, poverties, quarrels, and tears, and yet is able to rise above them, and to have the unitive consciousness in which he is able to see the B-realm [Being-realm], to see the beauty of the whole cosmos, in the midst of all the vices, contentions, tears, and quarrels.[10]

Although this distinction seems to be generally accurate, even here there may be examples of children who have experienced transpersonal levels continuously and in a totally integrated fashion (for example, perhaps certain child avatars).[11] In addition, it should be recognized that many children who have peak experiences, such as those reported earlier, do just what Maslow described; they rise above their own D-realm (level of personality development) and experience the beauty of the B-realm.

Maslow's point, in any case, should not be taken as an argument against children having transpersonal experiences, but only that their experiences may not be exactly like those of fully illumined saints and sages. Many adults have had transpersonal experiences that were transient, difficult to integrate, and hard to articulate. William James's *Varieties of Religious Experience* and Richard Bucke's *Cosmic Consciousness* are full of case studies of this kind. As we saw in Chapter 2, many of the childhood experiences related in this book compare very favorably in essential detail with the kinds of experiences described in these works. At the same time, some of the childhood experiences described in this book *were* articulated in a rather exquisite fashion (e.g. the child dreams and poetry) and many of the experiences, although not immediately integrated, *became* integrated in the course of the individual's lifetime (for example the image of the little flower and the Behemoth in Frances Wickes's dream related earlier). Childhood experiences of the transpersonal occur at a stage of the life cycle different from that of the fully integrated saint or sage. Yet many of the child's transcendent experiences seem to stem from the same divine origins, flow from the same higher vehicles of the soul, and emerge from the same transpersonal well-springs as those of more mature spiritual individuals.

One final issue remains to be discussed. Wilber and Maslow argue that the child cannot experience the transpersonal because "he is ignorant." The difficulty with this position is that it seems based on a conception of childhood similar to the *tabula rasa* image of Locke and the behaviorists. In this view the child comes into life empty of experience and in the course of life acquires those experiences necessary for possible later transcendence ("you can't transcend an ego unless you've had one"). This perspective ignores a fundamental principle of child development which has long been recognized in many Eastern traditions—that the child begins life with the acquired experience of many lifetimes or existences within its psyche.

We have already seen suggestions of this backlog of experience in the research of Ian Stevenson. Another example could be shared from the world of Tibetan Buddhism. In this tradition when a lama (spiritual teacher) dies, the elders go in search of a baby who will recognize the belongings of the departed lama. Chogyam Trungpa Rinpoche, a Tibetan lama now living in the United States, tells the story of how this took place in his own infancy.[12] Several items belonging to the previous lama were placed alongside several identical items not owned by the lama. When the baby correctly motioned in the direction of the authentic belongings, he indicated to the elders that he "recognized" the items and was thus in reality the reincarnation of the departed lama. This ritual presupposes that an infant can possess enough of a storehouse of memory from the previous lifetime to make the proper choice.

One needn't believe in reincarnation to sense that children bring into this life more than a blank slate. Carl Jung was one of the first Western researchers to acknowledge this when he noted:

> The pre-conscious psyche—for example, that of a newborn infant—is not an empty vessel into which, under favorable conditions, practically anything can be poured. On the contrary, it is a tremendously complicated, sharply defined individual entity which appears indeterminate to us only because we cannot see it directly. But the moment the first visible manifestations of psychic life begin to appear, one would have to be blind not to recognize their individual character, that is, the unique personality behind them.[13]

More recently, as discussed in previous chapters, psychologists and psychiatrists have accumulated clinical data that support the existence of a sophisticated consciousness before, during, and shortly after birth.[14] The findings of Stevenson, Wambach, Verny, Chamberlain and others lend credence to the idea that children, although new to this lifetime, are old with respect to a broader developmental spectrum. In this view certain children would qualify as having authentic transpersonal experience on the basis of having acquired access to transpersonal levels in previous lifetimes.

Such a perspective requires a reconceptualization of human development to account for the possibility of authentic

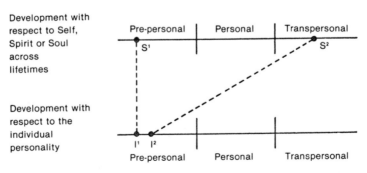

Figure 4. Childhood transpersonal experience[15]

transpersonal experience in childhood. Figure 4 suggests one way this might be done.

In this diagram, Wilber's concept of the life-cycle has been simplified into its three primary stages: prepersonal (subconsciousness), personal (self-consciousness), and transpersonal (superconsciousness).[16] Development is portrayed as a linear process: in Wilber's scheme transpersonal levels do not change back into prepersonal stages upon completion of the "cycle." The bottom horizontal line represents the individual developmental model adapted from Wilber. The top horizontal line indicates the more global evolution of the soul across many lifetimes or existences.[17] S^1 and S^2 represent individual souls with respect to their alignment in this broader sense. I^1 and I^2 represent those same souls with respect to their incarnation into specific lifetimes as individual personalities. In this diagram, S^1 has just begun its journey in human form whereas S^2 is a very old soul who has traversed the successive stages of human development (along Wilber's lines) and achieved transpersonal levels of experience over the course of many lifetimes.

The dotted lines indicate the path of each soul as it incarnates into a specific lifetime. Whereas individual souls can inherently belong to any stage, depending on their level of evolution/involution, *all* souls must and do begin at the prepersonal level in a given lifetime (e.g. they all take a physical/material birth wherein consciousness becomes embedded). In the cases cited, I^1 will have very little chance of gaining access to the transpersonal during prepersonal or personal stages of any given lifetime. I^2 on the other hand will have a much greater chance of experiencing the transpersonal during prepersonal and personal stages since these levels have already been navigated and transpersonal levels have already been consciously experienced in previous lives.[18] This scheme provides the beginnings of a developmental basis for transpersonal experiences in childhood that answers the objections of theorists who claim that the child has nothing to transcend.

It must be emphasized that, although from a "body up"

perspective the growth of the child seems to proceed developmentally along the lines suggested in Wilber's atman project (Chapter 3), there is a strong case for the potential interaction of *all* levels of consciousness *at any age.* Even in infancy there are the seeds of potential ego development. Piaget referred to these precursors of later development as "vertical decalages." For example, the infant's ability to grasp an object that has been moved away from it demonstrates the capacity to act consistently toward an object despite its changed appearance (different location in space). This early ability presages a later development in middle childhood when children can internally represent objects from a variety of perspectives (e.g. can mentally place themselves in the shoes of another person and imagine how an object looks from that point of view).[19] Likewise, there is recent evidence of an infant's ability to discriminate colors, shapes, forms, moods, sounds, and other stimuli while still in the womb or during the first days of life. This suggests that skills that will be used later during personal/egoic stages are already being put into practice at a rudimentary level in this early prepersonal stage of development.[20]

It also seems true that the infant, although embedded in a prepersonal fusion with the mother, may experience transpersonal glimmerings which are foreshadowings of later spiritual growth and attainment. Erich Neumann, whose concept of uroboros was borrowed by Wilber in his description of the "pre-personal," spoke of the uroboros state as consisting of both maternal and *paternal* elements. Wilber seems to have emphasized the maternal aspect of the uroboros in his discussion of "pre-personal fusion," while the paternal aspects were downplayed. This neglect was understandable, for according to Neumann, "the paternal side of the uroboros . . . is far harder to visualize than the maternal side."[21] Neumann writes:

> Although the ego experiences—and must experience—the uroboros as the terrible dark power of the unconscious, mankind does not by any means associate this stage of its preconscious existence only with feelings of dread and drowsiness. Even if, for the conscious ego, light and consciousness cleave together, like darkness and unconscious-

ness, man still has inklings of another and, so he thinks, a deeper "extraworldly" knowledge . . . [22]

Neumann says that this knowledge is both preworldly, *and* postconscious: "This is what the Jewish midrash means when it ascribes knowledge to the unborn babe in the womb, saying that over its head there burns a light in which it sees all the ends of the world."[23] This implies that transpersonal perception occurs at the same point in development as prepersonal embeddedness. It would appear, then, that Wilber's assignment of prepersonal and transpersonal to opposite ends of the life span is based on inaccurate and linear assumptions of human development. The deeper truth suggests that pre- and trans- are linked just as inevitably as the uroboric serpent links up with its own self.[24]

To balance what I have said above, let me underline the importance of the "pre/trans fallacy" in clarifying certain problems in human development which thus far have remained fuzzy. It is important that the primitive, preconscious experience of material unity with the mother *not* be confused with spiritual consciousness, just as it is important that authentic cases of mystical experience in adulthood not be reduced to prepersonal status. Yet by the same token, it is equally important that we not reduce authentic mystical states experienced by the infant or child. Otherwise, we are doing the same thing to the child's spiritual life that Freud and his followers have done to adult mystical experiences. By now it should be apparent that there is a world of difference between the kind of extraordinary peak experiences described thus far in this book and the sort of primal and diffused experiences of unbounded maternal fusion suggested, for example, in the psychoanalytic literature.

The real value of Wilber's "pre/trans fallacy" lies in its use as a tool for discriminating different levels of experience, regardless of the age at which they occur. That is why I shall proceed in the next chapter to apply the kinds of distinctions which Wilber has made between pre- and trans- levels, to the phenomenology of childhood states of consciousness. In this way I hope to make use of the pre/trans fallacy to link —not separate—childhood and transpersonal experience.

8

The Spectrum of Childhood Consciousness

Many children have visions easily and naturally. They do not distinguish between the visions of the mind and the visions of the eyes. They speak in the same way of both, without any special excitement. A daughter of mine informed me quite calmly that she had seen Jesus, "and He was leaning up against an apple-tree and He laughed and I asked Him to tell me a story." This vision remained with her all her life. In a sense, it was her life.[1]

Dr. Allen Brockington, Mysticism and Poetry

On September 19, 1846, two peasant children aged eleven and fifteen were tending cattle on Mount La Salette in the French Alps when they saw a bright light far off in the distance. Walking toward the light, they observed a woman who sat weeping. As the children came near her, she stood up and glided toward them, her feet several inches above the ground. The woman was dressed in white and wore a cap that radiated light. Roses of many colors surrounded her feet.

The woman gave a message to the children that the people of their region had made a mockery of religion and would be punished with a severe famine. She advised the children to practice their religion wholeheartedly and to spread her message among the people of the land. She then stood up, rose into the air, and dematerialized before their eyes. A glow remained for several minutes at the place where she had stood.

The next day when villagers came to the spot to investigate the story reported by the children, they observed a flowing stream at the site. Later it was claimed that these waters had miraculous healing properties.

The famine that the woman predicted did in fact come true, causing nearly a million deaths. Other things that had been told to the children by this radiant lady were reported to the Catholic Church but were never revealed.[2]

What was this experience? A vision? A fantasy? A miracle? A possession? The story of the children of La Salette raises an issue that this chapter will attempt to address: If indeed children are capable of experiencing the non-ordinary, how are we to distinguish these events from the more mundane "wish-fulfillment" and fantasy-ridden experiences of childhood? We are all familiar with the vivid imaginations of children. Children come up with all kinds of fantastic notions that clearly have no basis in fact. Yet this book has attempted to build a case for the belief that at least *some* of children's apparent fabrications are founded upon a deeper psychological or metaphysical truth. How then can we discriminate between what is pure imagination and what is authentic?

Contemporary child psychology, not believing in the reality of "other worlds" or higher levels of consciousness, has had no occasion to even ask this question, let alone answer it. Child psychologists ordinarily regard a child's experience of anything out of the ordinary as hallucination, fantasy, delusion, or in some other way connected with primitive levels of perception, affect, and cognition. In this chapter I will try to separate the wheat from the chaff, as it were, so that we can begin to make subtle distinctions between different kinds of childhood experiences. This may lead to a standard by which we can judge a child's out-of-the-ordinary experience—a dream, an image, a piece of artwork, or some other expression of the child's inner world. Such a standard would provide a means of interpreting that experience without ignoring or reducing its potential depth.

Several models proposed in previous chapters assigned different levels of consciousness to the human being. In this chapter I will present my own way of organizing childhood experience, based in part on the distinctions Ken Wilber has made: pre-personal, personal, and trans-personal. This "spectrum of childhood consciousness" will be different from the psychological or the metaphysical models discussed earlier in that I am not claiming these categories of experience are actually located in the child's psyche. What I propose is a way of understanding the child's experience, not another road map of the inner self. I suggest the following five categories for understanding childhood consciousness: prepersonal, subpersonal, personal, suprapersonal, and transpersonal.

Prepersonal

This category describes experiences related to the submergence of the child in a material/bodily connection with the mother/unconsciousness. We have seen in previous chapters how this experience is characterized by non-differentiation of physiological/sensorimotor/biological impulses, drives, and instincts. This is the realm of Neumann's maternal uroboros, Wilber's pleroma, Mahler's "normal autism," and Piaget's material self. In addition, this level of experience has roots in the archaic anatomy of the lower brain structures and the deep layers of the collective unconscious. Carl Jung alluded to this prepersonal level:

> The deeper "layers" of the psyche lose their individual uniqueness as they retreat further and further into darkness. "Lower down," that is to say as they approach the autonomous functional systems, they become increasingly collective until they are universalized and extinguished in the body's materiality, i.e. in chemical substances. The body's carbon is simply carbon. Hence, "at bottom" the psyche is simply "world."[3]

If we were to speak of consciousness descending into matter from a higher state, then this would be the place where the Fall has its nadir, where forgetfulness of one's true nature is at its most extreme, where consciousness is most

114

fully enshrouded or veiled. The prepersonal exists as the potential for material and psychological dis-integration at any age. The phenomenology of this category persists in the case histories of child and adult psychotics who feel the constant pull of the "devouring mother" archetype, the engulfing emptiness of open space, or the primal threat of chthonic creatures of the deep.

Subpersonal

This category describes the child's subterranean connections with nature and the family, linkages that appear to provide the foundation for psychic perception. This is the realm of visceral or "gut-level" psychology. It has been described by Joseph Chilton Pearce in terms of the bonding of the child to the earth matrix. According to Pearce, the child experiences a kind of "body-knowing" similar to that of animals who have an acute sensitivity to events in their environment that have important survival value.[4] This can be sensed by observing young children playing out in nature. They seem to have a deep intuitive grasp of geographical terrain, paying attention to geological details missed by adults with their more abstract minds. There appears to be a close communion between children and animals at this level, as the "boy meets dog" stories in our culture well illustrate.

The young child's link with the mother is all important here and has a psychic or telepathic quality to it. Erich Neumann and Jan Ehrenwald described this category in terms of a parapsychological symbiosis between mother and child. This underlying psychic channel extends to other family members and appears to continue in some form throughout life. E. Bruce Taub-Bynum, a family therapist, referred to the "family unconscious" as an invisible bond that links family members through shared experiences in dreams, telepathic communications, and other paranormal occurrences.[5] The young child is acutely aware of the familial/interpersonal field and exists in what Levy-Bruhl called a *participation mystique* with family members. As noted earlier, Jung frequently referred to the child's high level of sensitivity to the unconscious lives of their parents.[6] This subpersonal realm is the level where much of the instinctual and/or pathological familial unconscious is transmitted from parent to child (Assagioli's "lower unconscious"). Jung, R. D. Laing, and Taub-Bynum have suggested that the structures of this underlying system of transmission of pathology occurs across many generations.[7]

Phenomena associated with this category include many of the lower clairvoyant, telepathic, and psychokinetic experiences described in Chapter 2. As already discussed, the child's attunement to these phenomena can be ascribed to a high level of sensitivity to the etheric and astral fields described in esoteric psychology. Peterson termed the child's lower psychic abilities "atavistic" because they seem rooted in archaic or ancestral evolutionary structures. Children have little control over these powers and, as noted in Chapter 5, they tend to "close down" around the age of seven.

Personal

This category of experience describes the child's movement toward enculturation, socialization, adaptation to the collective, and any and all forms of adjustment to the cultural norm. The personal level circumscribes all models that speak of the development of the ego, the self (lower-case), or the personality. This is the realm of virtually all contemporary Western developmental child psychology. It includes Piaget's stages of cognitive development, Freud's psychosexual stages, Kohlberg's stages of moral development, Erikson's psychosocial stages, Loevinger's stages of ego development, Mahler's stages of individuation, and Goldman's stages of religious development.

Each of these models includes levels and stages that can be related to the previous two categories (prepersonal and subpersonal). For example, Mahler's stage of "normal autism" is essentially a prepersonal stage, and Piaget's stage of preoperational thinking shares certain qualities with the subpersonal category (although Piaget never recognized the potential for genuine psychic perception at that or any other level). However, these models properly belong in the personal category because they all share a common movement toward adaptation to the prevailing cultural reality. Piaget's level of preoperational thinking, for example, is only important within his model insofar as it serves to prepare the way for the more mature stage of concrete operations (it is, after all, only a "pre" stage). Other experiences that occur during preoperational thinking (for example the child's reports of paranormal occurrences) have no place in the personal category because they do not contribute to the movement of the child toward adaptation to the culture.

In this sense the culture serves as a screening device by which certain experiences are selectively cultivated through appropriate parenting and education, and other experiences are suppressed, ignored, or redefined into a more acceptable form (e.g. the child's valid perceptions of non-ordinary reality become "fantasies").[8] Experiences filtered out of the child's consciousness include not only many of those listed in the previous two categories but also those that pertain to the suprapersonal and the transpersonal levels, to be discussed below. What is left after non-ordinary experiences have been discarded is anything and everything that assists the child in moving toward a healthy adaptation to society, including fantasies, dreams, and imaginary companions when they serve to bolster ego strength. Our culture primarily encourages increasing levels of competence in mastering the skills of society (e.g. the basic skills of literacy), greater levels of independence and individuation from the mother and the family matrix, higher levels of abstract thinking, greater flexibility in interpersonal communication and connectedness, and increased ability to handle emotional states and cope with stress.

Most of what we see in the phenomenology of childhood (particularly at school age and beyond) belongs to the personal category. This is not to say that experiences from the other four categories are not happening in these children but simply that they are not *observed*.[9] Mostly, what we see going on in the lives of children concerns their efforts to internalize society's values, to develop skills and abilities that will give them a place within the culture, and to create for themselves the self-esteem and security that comes with a successful adaptation to the norm. To fail at these tasks is to risk psychopathology and a life of misery. It is impossible to ignore these tasks because most of what children encounter in daily life is geared toward instilling the prevailing view of reality of their culture. Because children's survival depends upon their ability to learn the "rules of the game," this is where most of their energy needs to be spent.

The personal category, then, describes the transmission between generations (parent-child, teacher-student, etc.) of skills, abilities, rules and meta-rules, competencies, learning styles, and roles that serve to perpetuate the culture.[10]

Suprapersonal

Childhood experiences that seem to come from a higher dimension of consciousness, yet are not quite the deep or peak experiences of mysticism and religion, fall into this category of the suprapersonal. They often appear to be psychic in nature, yet they are different from subpersonal (parapsychological) experiences that are more subterranean and earthbound in nature.

This category includes the child's visions of angels, spirit guardians, and celestial lights, as well as creative and intuitive inspirations, feelings, and perceptions. This is the place of Assagioli's "higher unconscious" or "superconscious" awareness. It is the level for certain archetypal contents of Jung's collective unconscious which are positive and wisdom-bringing in nature (e.g. Sophia or Isis as positive maternal archetypes). Higher aspirations, deep religious values, creative aspirations, and pure aesthetic and spiritual qualities are transmitted between adult and child at this level.

I feel that this area in psychology has been almost completely neglected by researchers. A great deal of attention has been focused on the ways in which psychopathology is transmitted between generations. However, almost no literature exists that seeks to determine how higher forces of health and well-being are transmitted through superconscious channels across generations. The image of the elder transmitting the spiritual heritage of the tribe to the child comes to mind here. There are numerous other subtle examples of the ways that parents and teachers unconsciously communicate love, reverence, beauty, compassion, and other spiritual qualities and principles to children.

Transpersonal

This is the realm of Wordsworth and Traherne, the peak experiences of Edward Robinson's studies, and many of the autobiographical reports of extraordinary individuals described earlier in the book. It corresponds to the cosmic consciousness of Bucke and the deeper varieties of religious experience described by William James. It is the experience of the child in connecting with the Self of Jung or the "higher self" of Assagioli. Metaphysically, it includes contact with higher dimensions of soul or spirit, the *anandamayakosha* or the Clear Light of Absolute Reality. Here also lie the child's deepest experiences of an essential core identity. This level also yields glimpses of an ultimate open ground of being or the witnessing of a universal panorama or cosmic spectacle.

Transpersonal experiences of this category, once encountered, continue to live within the child as a guiding light throughout the ups and downs of the human life cycle. They constitute the ultimate remembrance of one's real nature, and define the structure of one's life purpose or destiny. These experiences may come clothed in many forms: as a vision (Black Elk), a dream (Frances Wickes), a light (Yogananda), or an intuition from out of the blue (Jean Houston). In any case, their occurrence is extraordinary, their potential for healing immense, and their power to give life meaning unparalleled.

Unlike the other four categories, there is no specific vehicle for transmission of this level of experience between generations, unless it be in the context of a guru-disciple relationship. Children must experience this level alone, not as children but as pure being, identical in nature with the essence of Life itself.

The Spectrum of Imaginary Companions

The model presented above is intended only to be suggestive of the possible range or spectrum of levels that can be experienced in childhood. To some extent the categories of this model mimic the levels and stages of other transpersonal developmental models (e.g. Wilber, Vedanta, theosophy, etc.). Yet the emphasis here is not on stage-specific unfoldment: I do not mean to imply that the child begins with the prepersonal category and moves through each of the other four categories in turn. If there is any kind of flow or movement inherent in this model, it is of the twofold kind described as "body up" and "spirit down." The prepersonal and subpersonal categories delineate a coming up from the body, while the suprapersonal and transpersonal portray the child's descent from spiritual levels. The middle or personal category is the crossroads where "body up" and "spirit down" lines of development intersect. The personal category can also be what is left (as "ego" or "culture") after non-ordinary realities have been screened out. It should be kept in mind, however, that these divisions are entirely arbitrary. They emerged from my own personal process in coming to grips with some of the experiences described in this book. Many of these experiences might arguably fall into more than one category or require a category that has not been defined here. Yet I feel that the model represents a beginning. It can be useful as a tool in making distinctions between widely differing experiences at the childhood level.

The following common childhood experience illustrates how this tool can be used to discriminate between experiences that appear similar on the surface but in fact are quite different when looked at in greater depth. I have selected imaginary companions as a way of demonstrating the utility of this model. I want to show how the essential character of an imaginary companion in the life of a child radically changes from one category to the next. In certain categories the companion appears to be a pure fabrication, while in others it may have a metaphysical or spiritual reality that goes beyond pure childish fantasy.

A study by Ernest Hilgard of Stanford University reported that one in every six children involved in his research had experienced at least one imaginary playmate during their lives.[11] The peak time for this experience was between five and six years of age. The variety of imaginary playmates ranged from persons and animals to inanimate objects. Psychologists have typically attributed the existence of imaginary playmates in childhood to a variety of intra-psychic mechanisms that serve to help the child cope with the pressures of growth and change. As we shall see, however, imaginary companions serve not only a variety of psychological purposes but also appear at times to serve psychic, spiritual, or transpersonal ends as well.

In the *prepersonal* category imaginary companions are likely to emerge in the form of fantasies revolving around witches, threatening animals, monsters, and other primitive "devouring" archetypes. These symbols represent the uroboric mother whose pull toward the unconscious threatens the tiny ego of the child. Prepersonal companions also appear in the hallucinations of schizophrenic children, as for example in this case study of an eight-year-old girl who saw:

> . . . water balls which came to see her every night and bothered her during the day, such as when she tried to do her arithmetic. "They have keys instead of eyes. They want to know what I am doing and thinking."[12]

These primitive entities which emerged from the child's unconscious threatened to engulf her precarious hold on objective reality and thrust her back into a state of total dependency which is a hallmark of prepersonal consciousness.

In *sub-personal* consciousness, imaginary companions may come as a variety of unconscious projections of the child's still highly volatile imagination. However, they can also emerge possessing a psychic vitality of their own, as for example when they appear as fairies, gnomes, elves, sprites, sylphs, undines, or other forms of nature spirits. Folklore is rich in references to these "little people." Individuals such as William Butler Yeats and Sir Arthur Conan Doyle, the creator of Sherlock Holmes, were avid believers in nature spirits. Several books have been published cataloguing the different kinds of "wee folk" and speculating on their metaphysical reality.[13] Nature spirits are said to be associated with the etheric/astral levels of consciousness. They have been observed by clairvoyants to be active in the nourishment of all living substances from plants and animals to the growing child.

In other cases at the subpersonal level, the companion may be a discarnate entity or a person who has "died" and passed over to the astral realm. Jim Peterson, whose work with clairvoyant children was reported in Chapter 2, wrote about a four-year-old girl named Jill who gave a detailed description of an invisible "friend" named Sybil. Peterson reported that in one session Sybil was instructed to cross the room and "read" a number from Peterson's driver's license, which she did with uncanny accuracy (through Jill).[14] A similar study was reported by Charles Thomas Cayce, a child psychologist and grandson of the well-known psychic Edgar Cayce. The imaginary companion of the child in this study was instructed to go into an adjoining room and look at a telephone directory that had been opened to a designated page by one of Dr. Cayce's colleagues. Even the colleague did not know the page at which the book had been opened (to rule out the possibility of mental telepathy). The invisible imaginary companion, again through the child being studied, was able to give the correct page number, not just once but over the course of several additional trials.[15]

Finally, imaginary companions in this subpersonal category could be the poltergeists or "mischievous spirits" frequently found in the lives of adolescents. Most of these cases are connected with physical happenings and appear to be much more than imagination. Children seem to be tuning into a subtler level of energy and attracting entities that really are "out there" in some way.

In the *personal* category occur the most common variety of imaginary playmates. Just as in the prepersonal realm, the companions in this category of consciousness are truly imaginary. They stem from the child's growing ego structures and are in many cases instrumental in helping children deal with problems encountered in the process of development. In one way or another, they seem to assist children in adapting to their surroundings. If the child is separated from regular contact with peers, the imaginary companion may serve as a substitute friend to help the child deal with feelings of loneliness or abandonment. Frances Wickes suggested that imaginary companions may compensate for qualities missing in the parents. She cites a child's imaginary companion named Mrs. Comphret, who was "just comfortable and smiling and slow and quiet," in contrast to the child's real mother who was alert, quick, dominating, and insistent that things be done "at once."[16] Hilgard suggested that imaginary companions may play out a variety of functions representing multifaceted parts of the child's growing personality. They can represent the superego or conscience, unintegrated emotions, the observing self, the ego ideal, or even components of the child's creative potential.[17] One is reminded of the Bronte sisters who created two imaginary worlds—Angria and Gondal—peopled with a whole host of personalities whose characters eventually led to the writing of *Jane Eyre* and *Wuthering Heights* in these authors' later lives.[18]

Suprapersonal consciousness could possibly account for the vision described at the beginning of this chapter. There are many well-known accounts of similar visitations by the Virgin Mary, angels, and other spiritual or religious beings. Samuel Young reported several of these cases in his book *Psychic Children*. There is, for example, the case of Bernadette Soubirous whose story was made famous in the movie *The Song of Bernadette*. In this account the vision of a young woman about sixteen years of age appeared in a golden cloud to Bernadette and reappeared in several subsequent visits to the now-enshrined grotto at Lourdes.[19] For another example, in 1871 two brothers aged ten and twelve observed a vision of a beautiful young woman within a triangle of stars in the night sky in France.[20] Finally, in 1917 three shepherd children aged six, eight, and nine saw the image of a radiant woman near Fatima, Portugal.[21]

Closer to the present day, Young reported the story of a New Jersey woman who as a child was hanging up the wash with her mother when "the figure of an elderly man in robes holding the body of the crucified Christ" appeared to her, filling her with a great sense of peace.[22] Another woman from Texas related her childhood memories of "white-robed beings surrounded by light." The woman commented, "My reaction was always one of tremendous joy. There was always telepathic conversation between us."[23] Finally, I recall a woman in one of my own classes on child development who reported a childhood memory of a being of brilliant light that appeared to her above a tree. This being poured out a tremendous pulse of love that she said was greater than any love she had ever experienced before.

Each of these experiences has a psychic element—an otherworldly or apparitional quality that sometimes includes telepathic experiences. Yet they also bear deeper religious or spiritual insight that lingers long after the "apparition" has disappeared. Consequently, it seems clear that they should be differentiated from the subpersonal experiences reported earlier, which although suggestive of otherworldly happenings did not bring an influx of deeper meaning.[24] Yet because these visions did assume a materialized form of some kind, they remain at least in some sense within the psychic world and are not yet fully within what I call the transpersonal realm (using the word here in a more limited sense for the purpose of this model only).

The *transpersonal* realm holds experiences which may be less outwardly dramatic than those reported above, yet which plumb more deeply into the core of the child's being. The companions here are essentially symbolic expressions of the child's ultimate connection with spiritual truth. Frances Wickes suggested:

> There are companions that go with the child even unto old age. The soul, from earliest childhood, inhabits a world of brilliant darkness and numinous mystery, and from this world a friend may come, a friend who will companion the emerging ego on its never-ending journey toward consciousness.[25]

Wickes shared the story of a young boy whose friend was "little as a Twinkle and big as Pitch Black Dark." The boy reported:

> Twinkle is littler than a star but he really *is* a star. He is like a little spark that goes up from a bonfire, but that spark goes out and Twinkle doesn't. He *stays* . . . You know Pitch Black Dark can walk right into daytime. Then I have to think *hard* to see Twinkle. When I do see him sitting right in the middle of Pitch Black Dark, I am not afraid to tackle the thing I have to do and I know Pitch Black Dark is my friend too.[26]

Twinkle is very much like the "life star" of Wordsworth, whose glow contains the seeds of a person's ultimate purpose and destiny.[27] Pitch Black Dark appears to be a return to the prepersonal, when the blackness of unconsciousness threatens to overwhelm and devour. Yet it too is a friend to the child. It is, as the child says, part of Twinkle; for how can there be light without darkness? At this point we reach a place of mystery where prepersonal and transpersonal meet and where each is an expression of the same unending unity. This is the experience of Self, whether of Void or of Substance, whose living expression constitutes the heart of all spiritual/transpersonal experience.

9

Helping Children on Non-Ordinary Levels

Their carefree hearts reflect qualities that are divine by their restless pranks and blissful for their innocence. It is for you to see how far you can make use of this 'Divinity' in man, expressed through the child-God.[1]

Meher Baba

Perhaps by now you are convinced that children have extraordinary experiences, but you may wonder about the usefulness of all these non-ordinary events when it comes to helping real children in the everyday world. We have a very results-oriented culture and many of us have learned to grow wary of ideas that sound good but have little practical value. When a book like this comes along with concepts on everything from Jung and reincarnation to E.T. and sweet-potato eating monkeys, it is natural to wonder about the value of these ideas in the lives of children. This chapter, then, is a first step in defining that value. I say a first step because the implications of these ideas for parenting, education, therapy, and research are enormous. This perspective promises to do nothing less than totally transform the way we think about children. Short of this monumental undertaking, what I want to do here is to offer a few suggestions for how this orientation to childhood can affect our attitudes,

126

whether we are parents, teachers, child therapists, child development researchers, or simply friends of children.

The Radiant Child and Parenting

As we have seen throughout this book, there are two sides to the developing child. One side is busy adapting to the contours of the three-dimensional world. The other side is at work remembering divine origins. The task of parenting, therefore, is likewise twofold in nature. Most how-to-parent books focus exclusively on the "body-up" adjusting part and neglect the "spirit-down" remembering part. *The Radiant Child* has emphasized the remembering in an effort to re-dress this one-sidedness. However, it is important to realize that the child needs *both*. A child who focuses exclusively on remembering will likely be labeled as autistic or schizo-phrenic. The child who is totally bent on adapting will probably live out life as a rigid, competitive, status-seeking, achievement-oriented adult. An integrative approach to parenting will acknowledge the child's spiritual origins and help the child incorporate that knowledge in very practical ways in the objective world. Here are some suggestions:

• Take a few moments out of every day and simply focus on your child as a being who is larger than the small ego which is forming. The theosophist George Arundale once said of the child: "There is much more of him there than you can see."[2] You can call this larger something potential, emergent unconscious, higher vehicles of the soul, Self, or anything else. The point is that this larger nature is more than a quaint metaphor: it is a living reality. Recognizing this can lead to a new level of respect for your children and allow you to see things in their words and actions that you never saw before.

• This broader perspective can help you to let go of your children and allow them to grow according to their own unique rhythms and patterns of growth. The view described in this book gives empirical support to Kahlil Gibran's famous statement about children: "They come through you but not from you."[3] The physical/biological body of the child did indeed come from the body of the mother and genetic encodement of the parents, and the child's physical, emotional, and mental worlds are sustained and nourished by that relationship and the broader influence of culture. But the spirit or soul of the child came from elsewhere. Although it is *part* of the physical, emotional and mental relationship with the parents, the soul does not belong solely to that relationship but exists with respect to a much broader, even eternal, frame of reference.

Recognizing this can help parents to be more detached from the daily stresses and strains of dealing with the emotional tangles that come from the child's emerging ego. Your role can change to that of serving as an attendant to one who is passing through your life, rather than your being the person upon whom the child's whole destiny revolves.

• This spiritual perspective of the child can assist you in helping your children make the frequently difficult transition between worlds, from the spiritual to the earthly. Children are coming from levels of being where there is a very different kind of logic, a different way of getting about (without a physical body), and a different kind of sensory-perceptual experience. As Hazrat Inayat Khan pointed out, the infant is "accustomed to much finer music than we can conceive."[4]

Look at the ways in which this understanding of the child as a being in transition can help explain their problems in a new way. For example, if your child is hyperactive, consider what Rudolf Steiner had to say about the newly arrived soul of the child:

> Suppose all you clever and well brought-up people were suddenly condemned to remain always in a room having a temperature of 144° Fahrenheit. You couldn't do it! It is even harder for the spirit of the child, which has descended from the spiritual worlds, to accustom itself to earthly conditions. The spirit, suddenly transported into a completely different world, with the new experience of having a body to carry about, acts as we see the child act [boisterous, awkward, hyperactive, etc.].[5]

This recognition may not make the child's hyperactivity go away, but your own deeper understanding of the child's situation can begin the process of soothing and calming.

• Pay attention to the stories and dreams your child tells you. Don't simply dismiss them all as pure fantasy (although they frequently may be just that). It is possible that the child is speaking symbolically about his or her experience of non-ordinary realms. As mentioned before, part of the reason that we don't hear more about non-ordinary experiences in childhood is because adults tend to suppress, ignore, or reduce these experiences in children. An adult in Edward Robinson's study cited earlier observed: "One learned to be careful what one told one's parents."[6] An individual in Annette Hollander's survey reported: "I found out it was O.K. to listen to talks about Jesus [in church] but not to be talked to by Jesus."[7] Other adults reporting transcendent experiences in childhood remembered the pain of having an adult brand their experiences as lies, delusions, or daydreaming. Because children want so badly to win their parent's love, they naturally sacrifice their own perceptions and learn to say what they do not feel. Yet all too often, with this sacrifice comes an abandonment of their own deeper Self.

This does not mean that you should encourage or probe deeply into the child's world when non-ordinary experiences are reported. This can be as harmful as ignoring or repressing the experiences. Charles Thomas Cayce reported that in his youth parapsychologists came from near and far to "test" him to see if he had inherited the abilities of his well-known clairvoyant grandfather Edgar Cayce. He perceived these visits as very intrusive. In one case he was "bribed" by a parapsychologist to say that he saw strange colors and lights! He simply wanted to be left alone and allowed to live a normal childhood.[8]

When children do see strange colors, lights, and visions, these can be very bothersome and interfere with the child's need to focus on the here-and-now. In such cases the task of the parent may be to help *ground* the child in objective real-

129

ity. As one mother who was psychic as a child put it: "If I'm working with a child at school and he sees a blob drifting across his desk, I say O.K., what does this blob look like? Where is it now? Fine. Now have you finished your homework?"⁹ The perception is acknowledged, it is described, no further attention is focused on it, and the child's attention is then directed to the task at hand (the adapting part of development). Whether the parent should spend more time acknowledging or grounding depends upon the child, the nature of the experience (whether psychic or spiritual for example), and the context (does it occur in a way that interferes with or in a way that advances the child's growth and development?).

• One way of acknowledging experience of the non-ordinary is to communicate with the child about this realm through fairy tales or other visionary children's literature. Jungians believe that fairy tales are actually allegories that describe the structure of the psyche on all levels. Children show by their delight in these stories that some part of their being hears and understands the hidden messages. When possible, *tell* the stories out of your own being, don't simply read them. Rudolf Steiner said that a great deal of the vitality of the story is lost when it is read.¹⁰ Parents should first get to know the story and let it mix with the juices of their own unconscious, so to speak, before sharing it with the child. (See Appendix A for a list of fairy tale collections and other sources of children's literature).

• Artistic expression is another way of acknowledging higher worlds within the child's being. Children who lack every other means of communicating "memories" will reveal them through painting, drawing, drama, and music. Since the nature of non-ordinary experience is essentially nonverbal, art is universally a primary means through which these levels have been revealed. This is especially true for children, who lack the sophisticated terminology of transpersonal psychology and comparative religion, but who can easily express the ineffable with a drawing, a sculpture, a dance, or a song.

• Provide the child with the tools through which to express

these worlds, but don't program them with exercises or activities designed to "evoke" the transpersonal. One consciousness researcher observed how easy it is for "new age" parents to project onto their children the contents of their own spiritual desires. Hence, instead of getting Johnny ready for Harvard Medical School, they are busy preparing him for spiritual enlightenment. There are many books today which have this flavor (e.g. yoga for children, meditation for children, etc.). Some of these activities can be helpful for some children some of the time. However, it is the attitude which one takes toward helping children grow spiritually that is of greatest importance. Charles Thomas Cayce reported how in his childhood he was put into groups with children of other spiritually aware parents and felt that there was "something fishy about it all."[11] Children are extremely sensitive to the intentions of their parents and will easily intuit whether they are being exposed to something because it is intrinsically worthwhile or because "mom and dad want me to do it."

• This leads to perhaps the most important parenting (as well as educational and therapeutic) principle of all: What you *do* is more important that what you *say*, and who you *are* is more important than what you *do*. The first part of this principle is understandable: children, as noted above, easily pick up on hypocrisy. This sensitivity extends beyond words and actions to thoughts, intentions, feelings, and ways of being. This is especially true during the first seven years of life. As observed, children during this time are extremely vulnerable to the psychic atmosphere around them, so that moods and emotions can have an immense impact.

Steiner and other esoteric writers, as well as mainstream psychologists, have noted how strong emotions, deeply implanted within the child, can induce physical and emotional illness later in life. Somatic systems of psychotherapy such as Rolfing, bioenergetics, and Reichian work have borne this out in their discoveries of how emotional trauma becomes encoded within bodily tissue. Yet children can be affected as powerfully by thought and intention as by strong emotions.

Many parents are aware of the importance of not blowing

up in anger at a child. Yet few parents realize that their *thoughts* can also harm the child. Recall what Jung said about how children can be powerfully affected by the lives that their parents *haven't lived*.[12] In the unspoken words, the hidden frustrations, the family secrets, and the negative inner attitudes that masquerade as "proper behavior," the child is subtly molded.

• Fortunately, this works the other way as well. Children are powerfully affected by the positive dimensions of an adult's inner life. Even when the parent seems not to have said or done the "right" thing, if the intention was pure and backed up by a life of right living, then the child will probably be well nurtured by this unseen aspect of the parent's deeper nature.

As already mentioned, subtle transmissions can occur between parent and child (or teacher and student, therapist and client, etc.) on suprapersonal levels. Just as the lower unconscious can transmit hang-ups and neurosis, the higher unconscious can transmit inspiration, courage, love, and many other high ideals that flow from spiritual realms. This is an important concept. Frequently parents feel guilty about their child-raising methods. They read "how-to" books and usually discover that they have been doing things "all wrong" for years. However, from the standpoint of transpersonal parenting, it doesn't make any difference what methods of child-rearing you use as long as they are a product of your deepest intuitions of how to help your child, and as long as you yourself are striving to become the best person that you know how to be. Often the realization that one doesn't have to be "the perfect parent" (or the perfect teacher or therapist) helps to defuse pressure and guilt, opening the way to more natural (and thereby more effective) ways of parenting, ways that reflect who you are as a parent right now.

• Recently a parent related the following to me: "I really want to nurture my child's spiritual life. Should I send him to church and have him attend Sunday school? I feel torn about this because my own religious training was pretty meaningless and I don't want my child to go through what I went through. On the other hand, I really feel as if I'm not providing my child with any structure as far as religious training and wonder if a formal church affiliation would help. What should I do?"

This is a complex question. Formal religious instruction for many children is simply another adaptation they must make to culture and can be boring, painful, and irrelevant to their deeper spiritual needs.[13] My own early memories of Sunday School have much more to do with cookies and Kool Aid than with spirituality. On the other hand, religious training, whether at home or at church, can be the foundation stone upon which the child moves through life as a spiritual being. The experiences that a child has during a family prayer time or in a meaningful dialogue with a member of the clergy can tap higher spiritual levels of the unconscious. Which of these two directions is taken depends not on the form of religious instruction, but rather upon the deeper intentions and attunement of the parent or church figure. Erik Erikson, the noted child psychoanalyst, put his finger on the heart of the matter when he said:

> The clinician can only observe that many are proud to be without religion whose children cannot afford their being without it. On the other hand, there are many who seem to derive a vital faith from social action or scientific pursuit. And again, there are many who profess faith, yet in practice breathe mistrust both of life and man.[14]

Thus, the important question is not "Should I send my child to church?" but "What is my *own* attitude toward life's great mysteries and how do I want to communicate with my child about these things?" The answer reached will be different in each case and may involve church affiliation or family-created rituals. On the other hand, one's solution may have more to do with living life according to one's deepest principles and letting the child learn from that.

The Radiant Child and Education

Education has come to mean acculturation and is synonymous in many cases with the closing down of the child's awareness of a deeper reality. The child enters school and is exposed to abstract thinking, homework, competitive peer relationships, rote drill, and long teacher soliloquies. These activities not only strain the eyes, ears, hands, and bodies of young children, they also squeeze out the richness of non-ordinary experience. The true meaning of education (from the Latin *educare* to draw out) implies that these inner worlds not be forgotten by the teacher but in some way tapped and integrated into everyday life. Teachers need to recognize the importance of introducing into their curriculum and into their own teaching styles ideas and principles that will help draw forth this process in the lives of their students. Here are a few suggestions:

• Avoid pushing children into abstract thinking too soon. Several "transpersonal educators" who were seers in their own right, including Rudolf Steiner, Sri Aurobindo, and Hazrat Inayat Khan, emphasized that children should generally not be exposed to formal schooling until around the age of seven. Granted that this is impractical in this day and age, teachers can have enough sensitivity to make sure that children, especially in the early grades, are exposed to activities that are connected in meaningful ways to the child's inner psyche. The Waldorf Education curriculum designed by Rudolf Steiner embodies in a very real way the connection of academic skills with the deeper need of the child for imaginative experience, artistic expression, and the evocation of feeling and rhythm. Children are taught reading, writing, and arithmetic through storytelling, painting, drama, and other artistic means. More recently the field of transpersonal education has promoted a whole range of methods and materials for utilizing metaphor, myth, movement, and other creative approaches to learning in conjunction with the more linear basic skills (See Appendix B for a list of books that follow this approach). These activities can feed the "remembering" side of childhood and at the same time help children adapt to the world by making it easier for them to learn the competencies required by society.

• At the same time, teachers should discriminate between

"new age" activities that are useful and those that seem helpful on the surface but are really not valuable in a deeper sense. For example, meditation and guided imagery activities for children are currently very popular in classrooms. Yet I personally feel that having children close their eyes and imagine lights or images may not meet their deeper needs as growing individuals.

I once wrote a well-known eductor of my excitement about the new types of meditation and guided imagery experiences that were then becoming available. He wrote back saying that these activities—while seeming to help children relax—were just giving them another thing to worry about, another thing they had to learn to do. That made sense to me. If a child spontaneously shows a desire to meditate (as in the case of the Mother as a child, reported in Chapter 2) that is one thing. However I sense that formal meditation and guided imagery activities may teach children to dissociate their imagination from their feelings, bodies, and outer perceptions. With a teacher telling them what to see, think, or feel during these activities, children may also be learning to dissociate themselves from their own will.[15] I am reminded of what Hazrat Inayat Khan said about guided imagery for children, sixty years before it became popular in this country:

> Once I visited a school of thought-culture. They had made a new system, and I went to see it. There were ten or twelve children standing, and the teacher said, "Look what is there here?" There was nothing but a plain board before them. One child says, "A lily," The teacher says "All right." To another child he says, "Look, what is here?" The other child looks and says "A red rose." The teacher is satisfied . . . . And then he asks another child to tell what is there, and the child says "I do not see anything." I thought to myself, "He is the one who has some sense, for he did not tell a lie."[16]

Inayat Khan felt that this kind of training could only lead to a culture of mediums. He suggested helping the child focus on *real* flowers so that they could appreciate natural beauty.

135

Young children really don't need to be taught how to meditate. They already meditate when they become totally involved in an activity, a perception, or a relationship. Maria Montessori called this facility of the child "the absorbent mind." Children can be helped to retain this facility of absorption in natural ways that engage their whole being in activities such as storytelling, drama, walks in nature, and movement activities.

• Don't think that exercises and activities are the only way to connect with your students on transpersonal levels. I was tremendously frustrated in my own teaching career because I felt I was not doing enough "transpersonal curriculum." I would get upset when the activities that I did try did not work out. I would get angry at the kids for depriving me of the opportunity of becoming a "true" transpersonal educator.

As it turned out, the real transpersonal moments did not come in the middle of a dream seminar or during a myth-making activity. They generally came at an unexpected time when something special happened between myself and my students. One time I wrote a song for a child whose parents were going through a painful divorce. There were times when I was suffering inwardly from some personal problem and the kids, picking up on that, were especially kind to me that day. Somehow at moments like these a special higher something was occurring at some unseen levels between myself and my student.

• Once you realize that this level does exist in your relationship with your students, nourish that channel of communication. Even though prayer in the public classroom is prohibited, there is nothing to forbid you from praying silently for your students, or in some other way creating a silent bond on a higher level between you and the class. One vehicle of spiritual bonding that was very powerful in my own teaching revolved around a song made popular by the Carpenters: "Bless the Beasts and the Children." The words went in part, "Light their way when the darkness surrounds them. Give them love, let it shine all around them." This song, which I sometimes played before going off to school, drew forth images of protection and light surrounding the classroom and evoked from me my own deepest sense of purpose related to my vocation as a teacher of children.

The Radiant Child and Psychotherapy

The two dominant methods for therapy with children in this culture are psychodynamic (Freudian-based) and behavioral. This means that when a child comes into a therapy room with a problem, the therapist is likely to either ignore the child's inner life (behavioral approach) or interpret the child's problems in terms of a fairly mechanistic view of the intrapsychic self (Freudian approach). Recently some attention has been given to cognitive and humanistic approaches to working with children (see for example Violet Oaklander's book *Windows to Our Children* in Appendix B). However, with the exception of work done by a few Jungian child psychotherapists such as Dora Kalff, Edith Sullwold, and Frances Wickes, there is little in the way of transpersonal approaches to helping children. Part of the problem is that most transpersonal psychologists have not even considered childhood as transpersonal and have generally relied upon conventiona' maps of child development (Freud, Piaget, Erikson, Mahler, etc.) to help them in their work with troubled children. However, since this book has shown that there is a strong case to be built for a transpersonal domain in childhood, there is a need for a corresponding movement toward creating transpersonal models of child psychotherapy that acknowledge and make use of the higher nature of the child. Here are a few suggestions for ways to begin:

• Use active methods of therapy that allow children to express their inner world in a variety of ways: sand tray therapy, drama, art and movement therapy, etc. Watch for symbols that occur in the course of a child's play that point toward the non-ordinary. Sand tray therapy is particularly suitable for this because of the variety of symbols a child can use to build "a world." Provide a range of images, from plastic primeval monsters to miniatures of people in a variety of cultures and occupations to religious icons and symbols. These images supply children with the materials to build the prepersonal, personal, and transpersonal dimensions of their existence.

• Watch for a moment during therapy that reveals deeper aspects of the child's psyche. When it occurs it can signify a turning point in the therapy. It can represent a point of contact with a deeper level in the psyche that enables the child to move beyond obstacles to growth. As Edith Sullwold, a Jungian child therapist, noted:

> It can appear symbolically (in images of centering or balancing, or as a circle or a square) in a dream, in a drawing, in a clay piece, or in a song or dance. This experience is a numinous moment in therapy. It can reenergize and direct the course of the growth process in true relation to the individual nature of the child. The harmonizing effect of this moment provides in itself a healing factor for a child.[17]

• Develop the ability to differentiate among the five categories of childhood consciousness described in Chapter 8: prepersonal, subpersonal, personal, suprapersonal, and transpersonal. When the child brings in a new experience —for example an imaginary companion—you will then be in a position to decide what aspect of the child is involved. This will determine your own response in therapy. You would not work with a child having hallucinations of water balls in the same way that you would work with a child who had experienced a vision of a divine presence. The latter may only be imagination, but unfortunately, too many child therapists today would automatically treat them both as delusions. A transpersonal approach to child therapy recognizes, as Ken Wilber has rightly pointed out, the vast difference between "pre-" experiences and "trans-" experiences within the psyche.

• The ability of child therapists to make differentiations depends a great deal on their own attunement to these different categories of experience. Fortunately or unfortunately as the case may be, there is no transpersonal version of the DSM-III (Diagnostic and Statistical Manual) available to establish objective criteria for what constitutes authentic non-ordinary experience. Only the therapist's intuition and sensitivity to non-ordinary reality can determine how to interpret and work with a given child's experience.

• As with parents and teachers, the need is great for therapists to work on their own growth and personal unfoldment. You might keep a journal of events (dreams, synchronicities, etc.) that can help reveal patterns of interaction from non-ordinary levels that occur between you and your client.

• A key word for the transpersonal child therapist is *integration*. Children are emerging from a body-ego rooted in "lower" biological/instinctual forces at the same time that they are descending from a "higher" spiritual world. The power that is locked up in both these lines of development must be sensitively integrated with the child's movement toward greater adaptation to the world around him. In short, all five categories of childhood consciousness must be directed toward the goal of helping the child live a full and rich life.

• Pay particular attention to special groups of children for whom non-ordinary experiences are more frequent. This includes children facing catastrophic or life-threatening illnesses. Elisabeth Kübler-Ross, drawing on her own extensive work with such children, observed:

> If you talk to any five-, six- or seven-year-old child who has a terminal illness . . . he will talk like a ninety year old, like a very old, wise soul, with all the wisdom of ninety years of living. This happens even if the parents are unspiritual. Like this little guy yesterday who said to me, "I enjoy every moment of my life now. I can now go to toy shops and browse around, and I get as much enjoyment out of browsing as I had before from buying one of the toys."[18]

Another special group of children consists of those labeled autistic or schizophrenic. Ernest Pecci, a psychiatrist who has worked with over 2000 such children, notes that some of them still have one foot in "the other world" and have been unable to make the transition into concrete, objective reality.[19] The real task of the therapist is to help these children complete the transition so that they can learn the lessons and skills they have come here to learn. In order to help them in this way, it is important to understand their individual worlds, and in many cases these worlds are at least in part psychic and spiritual in nature.

Another group includes developmentally delayed or retarded children. Because they frequently lack the verbal, cognitive, and social skills necessary for an easy adaptation to society, they are forced to rely upon deeper-level skills and abilities, including a rich quality of emotional expressiveness, psychic abilities, and a profound spiritual sensitivity. I recall spending an afternoon at Fernald State School in Boston and visiting children who would spend their whole lives in a state of helpless dependency on others; these were the "mat children" who would never even learn to feed themselves. The quality of spirituality in that room reminded me of feelings I experienced while attending a Krishnamurti lecture or while visiting Meher Baba's ashram in India. I felt as though the larger beings of these mat children were there beside them pouring out love and compassion to all who entered.

A final group includes the gifted and supergifted child. As noted earlier Assagioli felt that these children are capable of deep spiritual insight at a very early age. In many cases such children see through the thin mayavic shell that society has woven for them. They stand and point at the "emperor's new clothes" while searching for something beyond the veneer of superficial societal standards.

The Radiant Child and Developmental Psychology

It should be apparent by now that current models of child development need to be modified or in some cases drastically transformed to accommodate non-ordinary kinds of experiences. As we have seen, contemporary theories of child psychology such as those of Piaget, Freud, Mahler, and Erikson are well suited to explain that part of the child that emerges from the biological/material plane of existence. They say nothing, however, of the child's spiritual origins. For this dimension of the child's growth we have had to rely upon the teachings of esoteric and spiritual teachers such as Sri Aurobindo, Geoffrey Hodson, Laurence and Phoebe Bendit, Rudolf Steiner, Hazrat Inayat Khan, Alice Bailey and Jiddu Krishnamurti, among others. In most cases what we have from these figures, while lucid and perceptive, still falls short of a comprehensive model of child development. The closest thing to a complete transpersonal developmental psychology reflecting the spiritual origins of childhood is Rudolf Steiner's system. As we saw in Chapter 5, his model of childhood, based on seven-year cycles, roughly approximates Piaget's stages of cognitive development. Yet it goes beyond Piaget in its appreciation for the more subtle energies that fuel the child's growth.

Steiner's system is sixty years old, and little has been done to update his conclusions or make them relevant to current trends in child psychology.[20] Clearly there is a need for Steiner's developmental psychology to be investigated and taken seriously by child development researchers. There are several important issues from Steiner and other transpersonal theorists that developmental psychologists could productively explore:

• Ian Stevenson pointed out that if children do indeed reincarnate from other lifetimes and other levels, this can help to explain several developmental problems that so far have baffled researchers. This view can help to explain why identical twins often show such different personality characteristics, why children sometimes have fears, prejudices, or preferences that can't be accounted for in terms of anything that has happened to them in their lives, and why parents sometimes have a particular attraction or repulsion to one of their children. (Stevenson suggests that they may have had a particularly close or stormy relationship in a previous lifetime.)²¹ Stevenson's rigorous methodology for exploring claims of reincarnation in childhood deserves careful study and represents a good model for how this kind of child development research can be conducted.

• Piaget's stage of preoperational thinking and Freud's concept of primary process need to be reinterpreted in light of psychic and spiritual experiences in childhood. Traditional pre-operational or magical thinking is usually regarded as a transitional stage of primitive cognition and emotion in the life of the child. In this mode of perception, the child is confused about inner and outer experiences, speaks paradoxically about phenomena in the world, and mixes his own feeling life with his descriptions of objective reality. An example of this kind of thought is animism. Piaget used this word to describe the tendency of the child to attribute the quality of life to "dead" things, as for example when the child considers a leaf blowing in the wind or a rushing stream to be "alive." Piaget regarded this kind of perception as immature and soon to be displaced by a more sophisticated form of thinking (concrete operations) where the child could clearly differentiate between animate and inanimate things.

A transpersonal approach to the study of preoperational development would agree that many inanimate objects are inaccurately given a quality of life by the child. However, it also argues that in certain instances, the child really is tuning in to the life quality or vitality of an object. As already noted, the child before the age of seven (the time of preoperational thinking) is psychically open to the etheric and astral realms or from a Jungian perspective, is sensitive to the contents of the collective unconscious. In any case, what the child is observing, whether a living archetype or an astral entity, may really be suffused with life. In this sense then, it is the child's sensitivity, and not his projection, that is responsible for the observed animism. Esoteric writers, parapsychologists, and even physicists have noted that rocks and minerals are suffused with a kind of vitality. Theosophical writers claim that they have etheric and astral counterparts. Spiritual seers have developed cosmologies in which consciousness evolves through rock and mineral stages. So if a child says that he feels the rocks are alive, perhaps in a sense he is right!

• Lawrence Kohlberg has developed a theory of moral development that parallels Piaget's theories of cognitive growth. In Kohlberg's model, children below the age of six or seven tend to operate from a basically selfish moral principle (e.g. "I'm afraid to steal candy because I don't want to get caught"). This idea coincides with Piaget's view (shared by Freudians and in fact by most child development theorists) that young children are basically egocentric, seeing things only from their personal point of view. While this perspective may be right from the biological/material perspective, it does not seem to always work that way with respect to psychic or spiritual dimensions. We have already seen that children can take a whole range of unconventional view points (e.g. Jill's "companion" reading numbers in a remote room) and can experience high levels of compassion for the universe. Recently evidence coming from more conventional psychological laboratories shows that some young children exhibit higher moral capacities such as compassion, empathy, and unconditional love.[22] These qualities are found only at the highest stages of Kohlberg's model and then only in adulthood. While Kohlberg's model is primarily concerned with moral reasoning, still the assumptions behind his theories will need to be re-evaluated to accommodate this broader view of children's moral capacities.

• A great deal of research has been conducted concerning the ways in which parents pass on traits and characteristics to their children. Studies have examined this issue in terms of genetics, psychopathology, education, and anthropology. However, as noted above, there is virtually no research showing how higher impulses—creativity, inner spiritual feeling, and inspiration are transmitted from parent to child. What little has been done is largely reductionistic in nature (e.g. a person develops creativity because of a fixation on the mother, etc.) This area represents a fertile field for aspiring transpersonal child researchers.

• The tools that will be used in transpersonal child research will probably differ from current research approaches in many ways. They will need to rely more on phenomenological, hermeneutic, experiential, and heuristic research methodologies, as opposed to experimental, clinical, and correlational methods. However, many other approaches can be adapted from contemporary child psychology. Piaget's own work is a superb example, for much of his research was generated from the simple act of talking with and observing children in their natural environments. This approach, taken from a transpersonal perspective, will allow researchers to listen to what children have to say about their own deeper spiritual lives without reducing those experiences or trying to fit them into some elaborate stage-specific model (which is a danger even with the transpersonal models presented in this book).

Many other issues need to be explored. For example, it is presently unclear how frequently non-ordinary experiences occur in the general population at the childhood level. Although I have presented several models for making sense out of some of these experiences, we still have a long way to go before we have developed appropriate research tools and theoretical constructs that can differentiate among the many different kinds of experiences described here. Ultimately, the recognition of authentic non-ordinary experience in childhood promises to provide a whole new dimension to the field of child development. It will require a reworking of traditional developmental models to take account of these experiences. This quest is not unlike Piaget's attempts to decipher the structure of our highest abstract intellect by following it back to its origins in infancy. So too, this adventure seeks to unravel the riddle of spiritual and creative life by returning to its source within the mystery of the child's inner being.

10

Savage or Saint? Addressing the Whole Child

Thou happy, happy elf! . . .
Thou tiny image of myself! . . .
Thou merry, laughing sprite!
With spirits feather-light,
Untouch'd by sorrow, and unsoil'd by sin . . .

But stop—first let me kiss away that tear . . .
My love, he's poking peas into his ear! . . .
Good heav'ns! The child is swallowing a pin![1]
Alexander Pope

Not too long ago I played my guitar for a group of students and faculty at the school where I am studying for my doctorate in psychology. I sang several songs that I wrote about childhood and spirituality. One was about a child's recollections of past lifetimes. Another was about how we pass love from person to person.

I finished singing my songs and sat down at my table feeling rather good about having shared these paeans of wonder and delight. Suddenly, a small child, perhaps three years of age, came barreling toward me yelling, "Push off! push off!" I was sitting in a chair backed up against the wall, and the child was attempting to communicate to me his desire to pass through this obstacle. As he continued to yell "push off! push off!" and brusquely pressed his body against my chair and the wall, I was startled out of my reverie. A little voice inside me said, "How dare he talk to me in this way! I'll make him say 'please' before he can pass." Then another voice countered, "So then you'll be the authority and make yourself a hypocrite after singing all those delightful songs." What I decided did not matter much for he had by this time managed to barrel his way through, leaving me behind, scattered and shell-shocked, in his wake.

I thought about this incident for some time. It seemed to me that this child had come into my life at that moment to keep me honest, to remind me about parts of childhood that I had neglected in my sensitive songs. These aspects of childhood seemed selfish, insensitive, power-driven, and almost brutal in nature. The child that came driving down upon me was a whirlwind of emotional fury, a powerhouse of instinctual force, a consciousness that seemed bent only upon the problem of how to get his small physical body through the material obstacle that I represented.

This event brought in focus for me what is essentially a grand paradox about the nature of childhood. Edward Edinger, a Jungian analyst, superbly encapsulated the nature of this paradox:

> On the one hand, [childhood] is a time of great freshness of perception and response; the child is in immediate contact with the archetypal realities of life. It is in the stage of original poetry; magnificent and terrifying transpersonal powers are lurking in every commonplace event. But on the other hand, the child can be an egotistic little beast, full of cruelty and greed.[2]

This paradox seemed even more evident when I thought about all of the images that humanity has generated around the nature of childhood: the noble savage, the innocent one, the blank slate, the polymorphous pervert, the demon-seed, the wonder-child, the selfish little brat, and the hope for humanity, among countless others.[3]

I have chosen in this book to focus upon images of purity, spirituality, and transcendence in childhood, while demoting selfish and instinctual aspects to prepersonal and subpersonal levels. However, I could not finish this book without stressing my intention *not* to present a view of the child as a split being, consisting of selfish layers, spiritual layers, and so on. If there is one thing about childhood that stands out above everything else, it is the child's *wholeness*. I am not speaking of spiritual wholeness. I am talking about a wholeness that includes *all* levels, high and low, in an undifferentiated unity.

Certainly as adults we can look at the child and sift out behaviors and attitudes that seem to us to be earthly or spiritual in nature. Yet the child does not, at least originally, perceive himself as a fragmented being consisting of five layers or seven levels or three basic categories of consciousness. The child lives in an ever shifting yet internally coherent world. This is a world where dark and light, body and spirit, earth and heaven have not yet been separated out. While as adults we can stand back and build mental constructs about spiritual and material lines of development crisscrossing each other, it is the child who stands in the midst of that process, and whose inner being is the cauldron within which these higher and lower forces are melded.

In essence, the paradox that confronts us is the universal one mirrored in *la condition humaine*. This paradox is reflected in our culture's own confusion about the relationship between dark and light, where for example, Lucifer whose meaning is "the carrier of light" has come to be known as an emblem of darkness and evil. It is reflected in our ambiguous attitude toward the physical body; some have sought to starve and beat it out of existence for the sake of heaven, while others have said that heaven itself cannot be reached except through it. It is seen in the diverse cosmologies of history, some of which regard matter as eternally separate from spirit, while others see matter as essentially compressed spirit seeking new ways of perfecting itself. Philosophers have reflected upon this question and answered it with paradoxes of their own, for example, Nietzsche's "One must have chaos within one to give birth to a dancing star."[4]

This paradox brings us back once again to the nature of childhood. How can we speak of a very young child as totally identified on the one hand with the physical body and all of its Dionysian instincts and at the same time as totally absorbed in celestial orbs and angelic radiances? Individuals such as Norman O. Brown and Wilhelm Reich have attempted to reconcile these disparate qualities by pointing to the holistic nature of energies in the child that reflect both spirituality and sensuality.[5]

These contemporary ideas have their roots in ancient traditions which viewed energy as primal and undifferentiated (e.g. kundalini in the Hindu tradition, fohat in the Tibetan tradition).[6] The child's nature in this sense is buzzing and humming to the resonance of cosmic energies whose poles are to be found in both heaven and earth.

Several mythological images contain this sense of the child as being between two worlds. Carl Kerenyi points to the boy riding a dolphin with a flower in his hair as an image which "seems to indicate a creature midway between fish and bud."[7] Likewise, the image of Pan as a half-bestial, half-divine being is frequently depicted as a *puer aeternus* or eternally youthful boy. A related figure in Goethe's *Faust* is the Euphorion:

> Naked springs a wingless genius, faun-like,
>   yet in no wise bestial,
> On the firm-set earth he springeth, yet the
>   earth with swift resilience
> Shoots him to the airy height.[8]

These images evoke Jung's own observations about the paradoxical nature of the child archetype as beginning and end, vulnerable and indestructible, preconscious and postconscious, temporal and eternal.[9] We are left with a sense of the child as both a dark, material, unconscious body-self, and a light, transcendent spirit-self. A paradox, but a psychic reality nevertheless!

Such contradictions become more real when seen within the context of human experience. We have, for example, Jung's own childhood memory of the subterranean phallus whose one eye shone heavenward amidst an aura of light, an image which is both of the earth and of the spirit.[10] Then there is the childhood recollection of Teilhard de Chardin whose memory of the genesis of his own life's work reveals a deep earthly spirituality as well:

> I was certainly no more than six or seven when I began to feel myself drawn by Matter—or more exactly by something that "shone" in the heart of Matter.[11]

Edith Cobb continued with a description of Teilhard's experience:

> He had, he says "caught" the usual child's religion from his mother, but this secret preoccupation was an entirely separate kind of "worship." It was worship of iron! He collected a whole series of "idols"—in the country a plow key, in town a metal staple, even shell splinters . . . . He states clearly that the early experiences sowed the seeds of his pursuit of cosmic and biological evolutionary history in later life and that his capacity stemmed from these inarticulate roots.[12]

This understanding of the unity of earth and spirit in childhood is essential if we are to offer children the proper help in their movement through life. The danger in any transpersonal philosophy of childhood is that the darker and more selfish attributes of the child will be ignored or sidestepped. This is often a problem in "new age" communities, where parents want their children to live spiritually pure lives and fight against any trace of selfishness or "low desire." Such an approach to child rearing invites catastrophe later in life. Children need to explore the whole realm of bodily feeling, instinct, passion, aggressivity, selfishness, jealousy, the gamut of emotions, high and low. Laurence and Phoebe Bendit refer to this need in pointing out:

> The expression itself may not seem spiritual to the adult mind—as when a small boy becomes a pirate or gangster, but it is a necessary stage in the spiritual development of the incarnated individual . . . . Any attempt to bypass it in the name of higher morality may do harm to the development of personality and invite illness, if not disaster. J. A. Hadfield has said that if a child of six or seven is faced with a tempting dish of sweets and is too honest to help himself to them when there is nobody to restrain him,

it may well turn out to be too great a moral strain for his years.[13]

Any attempt to impose upon the child an external facade which is a projection of the parent's own desires for spiritual integrity will only drive these "lower" needs underground, where as "shadow" they can sabotage one's future efforts by emerging in later life as neurosis, psychosomatic illness, or even psychosis.[14]

By the same token—and I continue to stress the need for balance—there is another kind of repression that can have its roots in childhood. This has been called "the repression of the sublime."[15] It is represented in the peak experiences, cosmic visions, and images of harmony and wholeness that are forgotten in childhood, covered over because they do not conform to the expectations of culture. Just as a repression of physical and emotional needs can lead to psychological or physical illness in later life, so too a repression of the spirit can lead to a more subtle but nevertheless devastating condition that causes the person to move through life with blinders on, so to speak. In this stunted condition, the individual finds satisfaction in cynicism, skepticism, and rationalization rather than through making everyday life sacred.

The radiant child is not a transcendent being cut off from body and emotions. He is like Whitman's ideal, an alive organism who celebrates himself at each and every moment in time. He is the epitome of the incarnated individual, a living spirit within a healthy and dynamic body. There was a deep sense of vitality in the child who burst into my reverie described at the beginning of this chapter. True, the child was insensitive and even brutal in his approach. Yet his was not the manipulation of the insensitive adult who seeks all too often to smother the spirit through deception and deceit. His was rather an alive and dancing brutality that slammed into my consciousness like an awakening force, asking me to take a look at my own lack of inner balance. Having danced this particularly forceful note, the child danced on to other vibrations as the evening wore on, some with equal vigor, others of more subdued tone. The selfishness, insensitivity, and brute force of his being seemed to be of the earth; the honesty and clarity in his approach seemed to be of the spirit. Where one left off and the other began is a mystery to me. Yet these two elements of being defined his existence as a totality.

All through this book I have attempted to paint a picture of the dual nature of the child. It seems more accurate, in light of what I have been saying here, to conclude that these two lines of development are simply different ways of looking at the same unified wholeness of being. A paradox? Of course. Yet it is a paradox whose ultimate solution is to be worked out, not between the pages of a book, but in the ever-changing unity of everyday life.

This is the essence of the radiant child. Belonging to both heaven and earth, the radiant child dances into our lives as a bridge between dark and light, body and spirit, ego and Self, the individual and God. The radiant child spans and sings this wholeness in every fiber. We would all be wise to listen. Even better to sing and dance along!

Appendix A
Annotated Bibliography of
Transpersonal Children's Literature

Fairy tales and classic fantasy literature are not only spiritual nourishment for children, they are also one of the best places to begin a study of the transpersonal dimensions of childhood. The list presented below is but a sampling of the wealth of material available to adult and child alike. For a much longer bibliography of spiritually oriented literature, see the "Fairy Tales" and "Children's Literature" sections of *Inner Development: The Yes! Bookshop Guide* by Chris Popenoe (Washington, D. C.: Yes! Inc., 1979). For a collection of excerpts from classic stories with accompanying interpretations, see Madeleine L'Engle, *Trailing Clouds of Glory: Spiritual Values in Children's Books.* Philadelphia: Westminster Press, 1985.

Alexander, Lloyd. *The Book of Three.* New York: Dell, 1964. Taran, an assistant pig-keeper, does battle with the forces of evil in an attempt to save his beloved land of Prydain. On the way he receives protection and assistance from unsuspected sources. Book one of the five-volume Prydain Chronicles, which are based in part on ancient Welsh mythology.

Andersen, Hans Christian. *The Complete Fairy Tales and Stories.* New York: Doubleday, 1974. Andersen's tales, while often strange or sad, touch deep emotional wellsprings in the young child's psyche and leave an indelible impression of the richness of human feeling.

Aquarian Age Stories for Children (7 volumes). Oceanside, Ca.: The Rosicrucian Fellowship, 1951. Plays, poems, and stories about dreams, healing, positive thinking, angels, fairies, etc.

Babbit, Natalie, *The Search for Delicious.* New York: Farrar, Straus & Giroux, 1969. A twelve-year-old boy travels the length of the kingdom to conduct a poll for the king on the meaning of the word "delicious." In the course of his journeying he meets a 900-year-old creature who lives at the very center of the kingdom, a minstrel named Canto, and a beautiful child mermaid.

Barker, Cicely. *Flower Fairy Books.* New York: Two Continents Pub. Group, n.d. Beautiful full page depictions of fairy folk, each accompanied by a poem. Books in the series include: *A Flower Fairy Alphabet, Flower Fairies of the Garden,* and *Flower Fairies of the Autumn.*

Barrie, J. M. *Peter Pan.* New York: Grosset & Dunlap, 1979. A beloved tale that can be interpreted on many different levels (e.g. never-never land as the astral plane; Captain Hook as the Shadow of Jungian psychology, and Peter Pan as the eternal child of mythology). Children enjoy it regardless!

Baum, L. Frank. *The Wizard of Oz.* New York: Ballantine, 1984. The classic that became a universally loved motion picture. A parable of the quest for self-realization.

Burnett, Frances Hodgson. *The Secret Garden.* New York: J. B. Lippincott Co., 1949. A child goes to live with her uncle on a country estate and discovers friends and an uncommon affinity with the living things surrounding the manor.

Carroll, Lewis. *Alice's Adventures in Wonderland* and *Through the Looking Glass* (one volume). Harmondsworth, England: Penguin Books, 1973. Illogical and impossible worlds come to life in these classic works.

Center for Attitudinal Healing. *There is a Rainbow Behind Every Dark Cloud.* Millbrae, Ca.: Celestial Arts, 1979. Written and illustrated by children facing life-threatening and catastrophic illnesses. Reflects a deep trust in life and love in the midst of pain and fear.

Center for Attitudinal Healing. *Straight from the Siblings: Another Look at the Rainbow.* Millbrae Ca.: Celestial Arts, 1982. Writings and art by brothers and sisters of children facing life-threatening illnesses.

Coatsworth, Elizabeth. *The Cat Who Went to Heaven.* New York: Collier Books, 1958. An artist's quest to depict the Buddha's funeral brings love, compassion, and a miracle.

D'Aulaire, Ingri and Edgar Parin. *Norse Gods and Giants.* Garden City, N.Y.: Doubleday & Co., 1967. Beautifully and naturally illustrated tales of Loki, Odin, Thor, Freya and other Norse gods and goddesses. Yggdrasil, the World-Tree, is a mythic description of the different levels of human consciousness. The D'Aulaire's have also written books on Greek myths and trolls.

Grimm's Fairy Tales, The Complete. New York: Pantheon, 1972. This edition includes an introduction by the well-known Irish poet Padraic Colum and a commentary by Joseph Campbell, the noted contemporary mythologist.

Jampolsky, Gerald G., ed. *Children as Teachers of Peace.* Millbrae, Ca.: Celestial Arts, 1982. A collection of writings and art by children on the theme of world peace. Includes children's responses to the statement, "If I were a teacher to the world leaders, I'd say . . . . "

Kotzwinkle, William. *E.T. the Extra-Terrestrial in his Adventure on Earth.* New York: Berkley, 1982. The book version of the movie E. T., based on the screenplay by Melissa Mathison.

Kübler-Ross, Elisabeth (illus. Heather Preston). *Remember The Secret.* Berkeley, Ca.: Celestial Arts, 1982. A book about death, travels out of the body, spirit guides, and love.

Kyber, Manfred. *The Three Candles of Little Veronica.* Garden City, N. Y.: Waldorf Press, 1975. A child's experience of nature spirits, angels, and other non-ordinary phenomena cast in a lyrical narrative format.

Lang, Andrew. *The Fairy Tale Books of Many Colors* (12 volumes). New York: Dover, 1968. This inexpensive Dover edition of Lang's collection of the world's greatest fairy tales is unsurpassed both in its quality and its accessibility. Available as separate volumes (*The Blue Fairy Tale Book, The Red Fairy Tale Book,* etc.).

Lang, Andrew. *The Arabian Nights Entertainments.* New York: Dover, 1969. A selection of the 1001 tales of Scheherazade, many of which are based on old Sufi stories. A dazzling world of genies, vizers, peris, and dervishes.

LeGuin, Ursula K. *A Wizard of Earthsea.* New York: Atheneum, 1968. A young boy goes to wizard's school and confronts problems surrounding the misuse of occult powers. Volume one of the Earthsea trilogy (which also includes the Newberry Award winner *The Tombs of Atuan* and the National Book Award winner, *The Farthest Shore*).

L'Engle, Madelaine. *A Wrinkle in Time.* New York: Dell, 1962. Adventures into time and space, with love as its final and enduring theme.

Lewis, C. S. *The Lion, The Witch, and the Wardrobe.* New York: Collier, 1972. Tells the story of four children who enter into another world through the back of a bedroom closet and have many adventures which make up much of the seven-volume *Chronicles of Narnia* (this is volume one). Other volumes include: *Prince Caspian, The Voyage of the Dawn Treader, The Silver Chair, The Horse and His Boy, The Magician's Nephew,* and *The Last Battle.*

MacDonald, George. *The Light Princess.* New York: Farrar, Straus & Giroux, 1969. A wonderful tale about the "grounding power" of human love. Illustrated by award-winning artist Maurice Sendak.

MacDonald, George. *The Princess and the Goblin.* New York: Airmont, 1967. Goblins in an underground kingdom threaten a princess and her subjects as well as a community of miners. The great-great-grandmother of the princess serves as an unfailing source of help in dealing with this menace.

MacDonald, George. *The Golden Key.* New York: Farrar, Straus and Giroux, 1967. Mossy and Tangle, two young children, journey to "the land whence the shadows fall," aided by an ancient and beautiful grandmother, The Old Man of the Sea, brightly colored flying fish, and many other remarkable creatures. (Illustrated by Maurice Sendak).

McDermott, Gerald. *Arrow to the Sun.* New York: Viking, 1974. Powerful spiritual parable of a young boy's quest to win his father's favor. Based on a Pueblo Indian folk tale. Simply written.

Morrison, Phil and Phylis. *Powers of Ten—On the Relative Sizes of Things in the Universe.* New York: W. H. Freeman, and Co., 1983. One of the most transpersonal of science books. A journey into the smallest particles and the largest galaxies of the universe. Definitely puts things in perspective! Based on another book (currently out of print) called *Cosmic View: The Universe in Forty Jumps* by Kees Boeke.

Nesbit, E. *The Phoenix and the Carpet.* Harmondsworth, England: Puffin, 1980. Five children go off on strange adventures via a magic carpet, with an ancient Phoenix as their friend and guide. By the author of *Five Children and It.*

Martin, Bette. *The Children's Material.* Miracle Life, 1979. Based on "A Course in Miracles"; consists of 51 lessons containing affirmations/meditations.

Nicholson, Shirley J. *Nature's Merry-Go-Round.* Wheaton, Ill.: Theosophical Publishing House, 1969. Another of the very few good transpersonal science books available for children. Elementary science experiments and lessons are given from a theosophical perspective (the cycles of nature/the universe, etc.).

Paulus, Trina. *Hope for the Flowers.* Ramsey, N. J.: Paulist Press, 1972. Delightful story of a caterpillar's sometimes arduous quest to become a butterfly. A parable of death and rebirth.

Saint-Exupéry, Antoine. *The Little Prince.* New York: Harcourt, Brace and World, 1943. A strangely beautiful tale of a sensitive little child-prince from another world.

Silverstein, Shel. *The Giving Tree.* New York: Harper and Row, 1964. A simple tale on the meaning of compassion.

Sisson, Ruth K. *Purple Dark and Starshine.* LaCanada, Ca.: Palm Publication Press, 1978. A bedtime story for children about the cycles of sleep and waking and their relation to the creation of the universe.

Tolkien, J. R. R. *The Hobbit.* New York: Random House, 1938. Bilbo Baggins goes off in search of the ancestral home of the dwarves where an evil dragon jealously guards a horde of jewels underneath a mountain. This children's fantasy prepares the way for the more sophisticated but nevertheless equally accessible trilogy, *The Lord of the Rings.*

Tolkien, J. R. R. *The Fellowship of the Ring.* New York: Random House, 1965. Volume one of *The Lord of the Rings* trilogy introduces us to Frodo and begins the story of his quest to protect the ring (acquired by Bilbo in *The Hobbit*) from the evil forces of Sauron. This adventure is continued in *The Two Towers* and concluded with *The Return of the King.*

von Heider, W. M. *And Then Take Hands.* Millbrae, Ca.: Celestial Arts, 1981. An anthology of rhymes, poems, stories, legends, and plays for children.

Wells, Benjamin, ed. *The Search for the King: Stories for All God's Children*. Walnut Creek, Ca.: Sufism Reoriented, 1976. Sufi followers of Meher Baba tell stories of the spiritual path to God.

Williams, Margery. *The Velveteen Rabbit*. New York: Avon Books, 1975. Love makes things real in this simply written classic.

Wyatt, Isabel. *Seven-Year-Old Wonder-Book*. San Rafael, Ca.: Dawne-Leigh Publications, 1978. Stories about nature, fairies, angels, from the perspective of Waldorf education.

Appendix B
Annotated Bibliography of Books
Relevant to the Study of Child's Higher Nature

Education

Sri Aurobindo and the Mother on Education (3 volumes). Pondicherry, India: Sri Aurobindo Society, 1972. These small pamphlets contain short passages taken from speeches and writings by Aurobindo and the Mother on the subject of childhood and education.

Bailey, Alice. *Education in the New Age.* New York: Lucis Publishing Co., 1954. A bit abstruse, especially for those unfamiliar with Bailey's work. However, contains a briefly described developmental model that may be useful, as well as futuristic suggestions for cultivating the different dimensions of the child's being.

Bennett, J. G., et al. *The Spiritual Hunger of the Modern Child.* Charles Town, W. Va.: Claymont Communications, 1984. A collection of lectures from a symposium held in London in 1961 on perspectives on spirituality and childhood. Includes Steiner, Gurdjieff, Montessori, as well as the Quaker, Roman Catholic, Buddhist, and Jewish traditions.

Canfield, Jack, and Harold C. Wells. *100 Ways to Enhance Self-Concept in the Classroom.* Englewood Cliffs, N. J.: Prentice Hall, 1976. Very practical activities for parents and teachers which touch on transpersonal themes (e.g. the ideal model, "who am I" questionnaire, the life line).

Fugitt, Eva D. *He Hit Me Back First.* Rolling Hills Estates, Ca.: Jalmar, 1983. One of the few books available which applies psychosynthesis principles directly to the classroom (100 Ways by Canfield and Wells (above) is another one of these). Includes samples of children's work, descriptions of how the exercises were applied, and suggestions for further reading. Exercises for development of the will, disidentification, and contacting higher wisdom.

Harwood, A. C. *The Recovery of Man in Childhood.* London: Hodder and Stoughton, 1958. One of the best introductions to the educational work of Rudolf Steiner. See also *The Way of the Child* by the same author.

Hendricks, Gay and Russel Wills. *The Centering Book.* Englewood Cliffs, N. J.: Prentice Hall, 1975. A practical book of exercises for expanding perception, getting in touch with the body, exploring dreams, and growing through storytelling. Includes suggestions for parents and teachers on how to apply these exercises in daily life.

Hendricks, Gay and Thomas B. Roberts. *The Second Centering Book.* Englewood Cliffs, N. J.: Prentice Hall, 1977. A continuation of *The Centering Book.* Activities for exploring communication, intuition, fantasy, and parapsychology. Includes the most comprehensive bibliography I've seen on transpersonal education (100 pages long).

Hendricks, Gay and James Fadiman, eds. *Transpersonal Education: A Curriculum for Feeling and Being.* Englewood Cliffs, N.J.: Prentice Hall, 1976. Excellent collection of twenty-four articles by individuals such as Aldous Huxley, Idries Shah, George Leonard, J. Krishnamurti, and Jiyu Kennet, Roshi.

Hendricks, Gay. *The Centered Teacher.* Englewood Cliffs, N. J.: Prentice Hall, 1979. Includes sections on avoiding burnout, raising self-esteem in children, cultivating responsibility in the classroom; also a section on "The Centered Principal."

Inayat Khan, Hazrat. *Education from Before Birth to Maturity.* Geneva, Switzerland: Sufi Pub. Co., 1974. Includes most of Hazrat Inayat Khan's transcribed lectures on childhood and education.

James, Walene. *Handbook for Educating in the New Age.* Virginia Beach, Va.: A.R.E. Press, 1977. Based on the Edgar Cayce readings, this booklet explores several themes in transpersonal education, including curriculum, the role of the teacher, and the purposes and ideals of education.

Jung, C. G. *Psychology and Education.* Princeton, N. J.: Princeton University Press, 1969. A collection of Jung's papers relating to children and education. Includes one of the few case studies Jung did of a child, "Psychic Conflicts in a Child".

Krishnamurti, J. *On Education.* San Francisco, Ca.: Harper and Row, 1974. A collection of talks between this renowned spiritual "non-guru" and students at two high schools in India. See also his *Education and the Significance of Life.*

Montessori, Maria. *The Secret of Childhood.* New York: Ballantine Books, 1966. Montessori's writings combine the practical knowledge of a medical doctor with the aphoristic wisdom of a mystic. This book includes chapters on walking, movement, and rhythm, as well as sections on the spiritual embryo, and psychic development. See also her book *The Absorbent Mind.*

Richards, M. C. *Towards Wholeness: Rudolf Steiner Education in America.* Middletown, Ct.: Wesleyan University Press, 1980. The best introduction of Rudolf Steiner's educational work for a general audience unfamiliar with Steiner.

Roberts, Thomas B. ed. *Four Psychologies Applied to Education: Freudian, Behavioral, Humanistic, Transpersonal.* Cambridge, Ma.: Schenkman Pub., 1975. Includes a collection of articles on a variety of transpersonal themes such as dreamwork in high schools, child development and bioplasmic forces, and parapsychology in education.

Steiner, Rudolf. *The Kingdom of Childhood.* London: Rudolf Steiner Press, 1971. A transcription of several lectures given by Steiner to Waldorf school teachers on a variety of educational themes, including curriculum, discipline, and the metaphysical dimensions of child development.

Steiner, Rudolf. *The Education of the Child in the Light of Anthroposophy.* London: Rudolf Steiner Press, 1965. The best brief introduction to Steiner's metaphysical approach to child development and education.

Taniguchi, Masahaau. *Divine Education and Spiritual Training of Mankind.* Tokyo, Japan: Seicho-No-IE Foundation, Divine Publications Department, 1956. Chapters on the education of children reflect a "science of mind" perspective that integrates Eastern and Western philosophies of spirit.

Parenting

Berends, Polly Berrien. *Whole Child/Whole Parent: A Spiritual and Practical Guide to Parenthood* (Revised edition). New York: Harper and Row, 1983. Integration of general holistic principles into everyday life; comprehensive source of books, equipment, etc. for parenting.

Carey, Ken. *Notes to My Children: A Simplified Metaphysics.* Kansas City, Mo.: Uni-Sun, 1984 (P. O. Box 25421, Kansas City, Mo 69119). In his preface the author conveys his feeling that children who incarnate into this world are due some kind of report on what they are getting into. What follows are Carey's own stories and metaphors to help translate "life" in this world to his children.

Da Free John. *Look at the Sunlight on the Water.* Clearlake, Ca.: The Dawn Horse Press, 1983. Subtitled "Educating Children for a Life of Self-Transcending Love and Happiness." Describes the child development theories and educational principles of Da Free John [born Franklin Jones], an American spiritual teacher.

English, Jane Butterfield. *Different Doorway: Adventures of a Caesarian-Born.* Point Reyes Station, CA: Earth Heart, 1985 (P.O. Box 1027, Point Reyes Station, CA 94956). A personal account of a woman's exploration into the implications of having been born non-labor caesarian. Suggests that transpersonal experience may be more easily accessible to individuals who have come into the world in this way. Foreward by Stan Grof.

Eyre, Linda and Richard. *Teaching Children Joy.* Salt Lake City, Utah: Shadow Mountain, 1984. Very practical suggestions, activities, and children's literature for preserving delight, joy, trust, confidence, interest, curiosity, and creativity in the child. Written by "super-parents" (numerous national awards for parenting and family life) of Mormon background.

Heindel, Max. *The Rosicrucian Principles of Child Training.* Oceanside, Ca.: Rosicrucian Fellowship, 1973. A pamphlet that briefly outlines Heindel's model of child development.

Hendricks, Gay. *The Family Centering Book.* Englewood Cliffs, N.J.: Prentice Hall, 1979. Chapters on meditation/relaxation, problem solving, communication, and family dreamwork.

Hollander, Annette. *How to Help Your Child Have a Spiritual Life.* New York: Bantam, 1982. One of the best practical guides for parents on spiritual and religious education for children. Covers a broad range of questions from "Are children mystics?" to "Should I teach my child to pray?" Several models of religious development are presented and compared with Piaget, Freud, etc. This book is currently out of print but is available from the author by writing: Annette Hollander, M.D., 16 King Avenue, Weehawken, N.J. 07087.

Kübler-Ross, Elisabeth. *On Children and Death*. New York: Macmillan, 1983. A practical and sensitive book primarily directed toward parents who are faced with the loss of a child. Includes information on support services and sources for further reading.

Milicevic, Barbara. *Your Spiritual Child*. Marina del Ray, Ca.: DeVorss & Co., n.d. Simple and straightforward guide for parents on nurturing the spiritual life of their children.

McCarroll, Tolbert, *Guiding God's Children: A Foundation for Spiritual Growth in the Home*. Ramsey, N. J.: Paulist Press, 1983. Combines Christian, native American, and Eastern religious views with contemporary models of child development, humanistic psychology, brain research, etc.

A Theosophical Guide for Parents. Ojai, Ca.: Parents Theosophical Research Group, 1981. A rich source of short writings from a wide range of esoteric thinkers, covers parenting, child development, education, fairy tales, etc. Very practical and informative. An excellent resource for the parent who is a student of metaphysics.

Psychotherapy

Assagioli, Roberto. *Psychosynthesis*. New York: Viking, 1965. No child development here, but a wealth of psychological information concerning the nature of the higher self that can be applied to child therapy issues.

Campbell, Joseph. *The Hero with a Thousand Faces*. Princeton, N. J.: Princeton University Press, 1968. Again, not explicitly concerned with child development, but a must for understanding certain basic patterns of mythic development that can be applied to the child's process of individuation.

Hoffman, Bob. *No One is to Blame: Getting a Loving Divorce from Mom and Dad*. Palo Alto, Ca.: Science and Behavior Books, Inc., 1979. Description of the Fisher-Hoffman Process (now called the Quadrinity Process) by its founder. This process is a spiritual psychotherapy for adults that uses visualization and emotional regression to achieve a reprogramming of early relationships with parents. "Spirit guides" are used as a vehicle for healing the "inner child" of the adult.

Houston, Jean. *Life Force: The Psycho-Historical Recovery of the Self.* New York: Delta, 1980. Houston's model of childhood and adult development is based in part on Gerald Heard's "Five Ages of Man." Includes experiential therapeutic applications.

Houston, Jean. *The Possible Human: A Course in Enhancing Your Physical, Mental and Creative Abilities.* Los Angeles: J. P. Tarcher, 1982. Includes a wonderful autobiographical account of the author's spiritual unfoldment in childhood, as well as several exercises for unlocking one's own "left-behind" possibilities.

Kalff, Dora M. *Sandplay: A Psychotherapeutic Approach to the Psyche.* Santa Monica, Ca.: Sigo, 1980. A Jungian orientation to the use of sand tray therapy with children, adolescents, and young adults. Includes several penetrating case studies.

Neumann, Erich. *The Origins and History of Consciousness.* Princeton, N. J.: Princeton University Press, 1970. Based on the idea that the development of the individual recapitulates the development of the species, this book is rich in mythological theorizing on the structures of childhood/early cultural consciousness.

Neumann, Erich. *The Child: Structure and Dynamics of the Nascent Personality.* New York: Harper and Row, 1973. More technical in its use of psychological terminology than *The Origins and History of Consciousness*, this book is concerned explicitly with child development issues, psychopathology in childhood, etc. Presents Neumann's stages of ego development.

Oaklander, Violet. *Windows to Our Children.* Moab, Utah: Real People Press, 1978. Primarily a gestalt approach to psychotherapy with children, this book contains an appreciation for deeper levels of the child's psyche, bordering on the transpersonal. Includes many useful ideas for parents and therapists, as well as a very good reference section.

Parabola, Volume IV, Number 3, August, 1979. A quarterly journal published by the Society for the Study of Myth and Tradition. This issue is dedicated entirely to The Child. Includes children's poetry, cross-cultural myths, art, and adult writings on the profound nature of childhood. Available by writing Parabola, 150 5th Ave., New York, N.Y. 10011.

Talbot, Toby, ed. *The World of the Child: Essays on Childhood.* New York: Doubleday & Co., 1967. The best collection I've seen of articles on childhood by mainstream theorists that have a hint of the transpersonal. Includes Ernest Schactel's fascinating paper "On Memory and Childhood Amnesia" (explores why adults don't remember more of their childhood). Other writers include George Groddeck (originator of the concept of the Id), Jose Ortega y Gasset, Melanie Klein, and Friedrich Froebel.

Verny, Thomas. *The Secret Life of the Unborn Child.* New York: Delta, 1981. A Canadian psychiatrist shares a wealth of medical research which suggests that the human being experiences a high degree of awareness while still in the womb.

von Franz, Marie-Louise. *Individuation in Fairy Tales.* Zurich: Spring Publications, 1977. An excellent series of lectures by a well-known Jungian analyst, on the deeper meaning of fairy tales. Includes a good description of the image of the Divine Child (pp. 16-19). Other books in this series include *An Introduction to the Interpretation of Fairy Tales*, *Shadow and Evil in Fairy Tales*, and *Problems of the Feminine in Fairy Tales*.

von Franz, Marie-Louise. *Puer Aeternus.* Santa Monica, Ca.: Sigo Press, 1981. Lectures on the theme of the eternal child, especially as it manifests in the psychopathology of the young adult. Includes a psychological commentary on *The Little Prince* by Antoine Saint-Exupéry.

Wickes, Frances G. *The Inner World of Childhood.* New York: Mentor, 1966. A Jungian psychiatrist shares a wealth of experience from her work with children and adolescents. See also the chapter "Childhood and the Friend of Choice" in her book *The Inner World of Choice.*

Child Development Research

The American Theosophist, Special Issue: The Flowering of Childhood. Fall, 1976. Articles include: "Aspects of Child Rearing and Education from the Edgar Cayce Readings," "Psychic and Philosophical Perception in the World of Children," and "The Child Within." Available from The Theosophical Society in America, P. O. Box 270, Wheaton, Ill. 60189.

Bachelard, Gaston. *The Poetics of Reverie: Childhood, Language and the Cosmos*. Boston: Beacon Press, 1971. Bachelard uses poetry and a phenomenological approach to study the wonder of childhood reverie. A unique contribution to the study of the inner world of the child. Offers clues as to how a research design for transpersonal child studies might be constructed.

Bendit, Laurence J. and Phoebe D. Bendit. *The Etheric Body of Man: The Bridge of Consciousness*. Wheaton, Ill.: The Theosophical Publishing House, 1977. One of the best metaphysical descriptions of the child's development from prebirth to maturity, though limited in its scope to the etheric field. Written by a psychiatrist and a psychic. Integrates Jungian concepts with theosophical ones.

Chamberlain, David B. *Consciousness at Birth: A Review of the Empirical Evidence*. San Diego, Ca.: Chamberlain Communications, 1983. A rather technical booklet that summarizes medical and psychological research pointing to a sophisticated consciousness before and during birth. Well documented.

Cobb, Edith. *The Ecology of Imagination in Childhood*. New York: Columbia University Press, 1977. A unique work that combines autobiographical studies, psychology, anthropology, philosophy, and ethology in a study of the child's intrinsic genius. Includes a listing of the Edith McKeaver Cobb collection of biographies and autobiographies of childhood, which is housed at Teacher's College Library, Columbia University.

De La Mare, Walter John. *Early One Morning in the Spring*. New York: The Macmillan Co., 1935. A wonderful collection of childhood recollections by some of the greatest English writers of the last 300 years. Unfortunately hard to find.

Evans-Wentz, W. Y. *The Tibetan Book of the Dead*. Oxford: Oxford University Press, 1960. A phenomenological account of the transition between death and rebirth rendered in Tibetan Buddhist imagery. Useful for gaining a sense of what a child might have experienced before being born.

Frommer, Eva A. *Voyage Through Childhood into the Adult World: A Description of Child Development*. Oxford: Pergamon Press, 1969. A somewhat conventional description of child development that nevertheless bears the imprint of Rudolf Steiner's educational philosophy. Includes photos of children and samples of artwork.

Hodson, Geoffrey. *The Miracle of Birth: A Clairvoyant Study of a Human Embryo.* Wheaton, Ill.: Theosophical Publishing House, 1981. Describes the development of the embryo from a clairvoyant's perspective. Includes a discussion of the role of angels in the prebirth and birth process.

Jung, C. G. *The Development of Personality.* Princeton, N. J.: Princeton University Press, 1981. Includes most of Jung's writings on child development and education.

Jung, C. G. "The Psychology of the Child Archetype" in *The Archetypes and the Collective Unconscious, The Collected Works of C. G. Jung,* Vol. 9, Part 1. New York: Pantheon, 1959. An extremely significant paper that outlines Jung's views on the meaning of "the inner child" as a symbol of wholeness within the psyche. Rich in mythological source material dealing with a variety of child images. Also found in *Essays on a Science of Mythology* (Harper and Row, 1963) along with Carl Kerenyi's companion piece "The Primordial Child in Primordial Times."

Montagu, Ashley. *Growing Young.* New York: McGraw Hill, 1983. Argues that it is an evolutionary advance for *homo sapiens* to have retained more youthful characteristics in adulthood (a process called neotony) than its predecessors. The first half of the book is quite technical and scholarly. The second half focuses on those aspects of childhood that are beneficial to the species as a whole (e.g. imagination, curiosity, playfulness, wonder, etc.).

Paffard, Michael. *Inglorious Wordsworths: A Study of Some Transcendental Experiences in Childhood and Adolescence.* London: Hodder and Stoughton, 1973. Examines recollections of adolescents and young adults. Classifies experiences on the basis of emotional qualities (e.g. fear, joy, awe, trance). Includes a historical discussion of the autobiographical recollections of C. S. Lewis, A. L. Rowse, and others.

Pearce, Joseph Chilton. *Magical Child.* New York: Bantam, 1980. Outlines Pearce's ideas about how culture tends to impede "nature's plan" for developing the vast potentialities within children. Integrates brain research, Piaget, and animal studies with Uri Geller, psychic children, and mysticism. See also *Exploring the Crack in the Cosmic Egg* (New York: Julian Press, 1974) for discussions leading up to this volume, and *Magical Child Matures* (New York: E.P. Dutton, 1985).

Robinson, Edward. *The Original Vision: A Study of the Religious*

Experience of Childhood. Oxford: The Religious Experience Research Unit, Manchester College, 1977. The results of Robinson's studies are presented in a narrative format that includes many verbatim accounts of adult memories of peak experiences in childhood.

Robinson, Edward. *Living the Questions: Studies in the Childhood of Religious Experience.* Oxford: The Religious Experience Research Unit, Manchester College, 1978. Continues the work of *The Original Vision* with in-depth interviews of selected individuals. Shows how their early experiences continued to nourish and inform their later development.

Selfe, Lorna. *Nadia: A Case of Extraordinary Drawing Ability in an Autistic Child.* New York: Harcourt Brace Jovanovich, 1977. An in-depth case study of an autistic girl who at age six was producing art work far in advance of her years, beyond even what would be expected in a precocious child of that age. Numerous illustrations.

Stevenson, Ian. *Twenty Cases Suggestive of Reincarnation.* Charlottesville, Va.: The University of Virginia Press, 1974. First in a series of five books presenting the results of Stevenson's research into child reports of past lifetimes. Extremely well documented. A model for transpersonal development research.

Wambach, Helen. *Life Before Life.* New York: Bantam, 1979. The results of group hypnotic regression sessions conducted by a psychologist. Individuals are taken back to the time "before they were born." Includes data from questionnaires, filled out immediately after the regression experience, on a variety of themes such as, "Did you choose to be born?" "Did you have any help?" and "When did your consciousness enter the fetus?" Suggests a higher level of awareness was present around the time of birth.

Wilber, Ken. *The Atman Project: A Transpersonal View of Human Development.* Wheaton, Ill.: Theosophical Publishing House, 1980. This book presents Wilber's synthesis of Eastern and Western models of human development, extending from the unconscious unity of the infant to the conscious transcendence of the fully realized spiritual being. Includes a series of charts correlating Wilber's stages of development with those of many other systems (e.g. Piaget, the Kabbalah, Kohlberg, Buddhism, Erikson, Vedanta).

Appendix C
Resources in Transpersonal Child Studies

Education

Ananda Schools, 14618 Tyler Foote Rd., Nevada City, Ca. 95959. Offers seminars for parents and teachers based on Paramahansa Yogananda's "how-to-live school" concepts of childhood education.

Auromere, 1291 Weber St., Pomona, CA 91768. Books and pamphlets available on educational and child-rearing principles of Sri Aurobindo and the Mother. Also books for children on the lives of Indian saints, Indian legends, etc. (distributor for Children's Book Trust of India). Catalog.

Baha'i National Education Committee, Baha'i National Center, Wilmette, Illinois 60091. Child/parent education materials available including "Child Education Teacher Training Handbook" and "Baha'i Parent Program."

Center for Integrative Learning, 1595 Garst Lane, Ojai, Ca. 93023. Use of visualization, guided imagery, metaphor, intuition in education.

Holistic Child Guidance Course, P. O. Box 92, Gonzales, Ca. 93926. Two year correspondence course taught by Sufi teacher Murshida Vera Corda, covering physical, mental, moral-ethical, interpersonal, and spiritual development of children from preconception through the school years.

Matagiri, Mt. Tremper, N. Y. 12457. Books available on educational ideals of Sri Aurobindo and the Mother. Also books for children. Catalog.

Mead School for Human Development, 202 Pemberwick Road, Box 1517, Greenwich, Ct. 06836. Model school utilizing whole-brain approach to learning (academics plus arts, myth, creativity). Preschool through junior high. Described in *Saturday Review* (September 3, 1977) and *Dromenon*, (February, 1979).

Meher School, 999 Leland Drive, Lafayette Ca. 94549. Model school run by Sufi followers of Meher Baba. WASC-approved school combines educational philosophies of Maria Montessori and Rudolf Steiner.

Oak Grove School, 220 West Lomita Ave., Ojai, Ca. 93023. Model school founded in 1975 by Krishnamurti Foundation. Preschool through twelfth grade.

Waldorf Schools. A list of Waldorf (Rudolf Steiner) schools nation-wide is given in Mary Caroline Richard's *Toward Wholeness: Rudolf Steiner Education in America*, Middletown, Ct.: Wesleyan University Press, 1980, pp. 195-197.

Teacher Training Institutes for Waldorf Education: Highland Hall, 17100 Superior St., Northridge, Ca. 01324. Rudolf Steiner College, 9200 Fair Oaks Blvd., Fair Oaks, Ca. 95628. Rudolf Steiner School, 15 E. 79th St., New York, 10021. Waldorf Institute, 23399 Evergreen Rd., Southfield, Mi 48075.

Universal Children's Gardens, P. O. Box 2698 Grand Central P.O., New York, N. Y. 10163. Network of organizations and individuals having as its goal "to place 1,000 local children's gardens with one in the capital city of every nation on planet Earth by the year 2,000."

Transpersonal Educational Consultants:

Thomas Armstrong, Latebloomers Educational Consulting Service, P. O. Box 2647, Berkeley, CA 94702.

Jack Canfield, c/o Self-Esteem Seminars, 17156 Palisades Circle, Pacific Palisades, Ca. 90272.

Jane Vennard, Box 289 Star Route, Muir Beach, Ca. 94965.

Parenting

A.R.E. Youth Activities Department, P. O. Box 595, Virginia Beach, Va. 23451. The childhood education arm of the Association for Research and Enlightenment (based on Edgar Cayce's work). Publishes a quarterly newsletter, "All God's Children," for educators and parents. Also distributes a series of pamphlets entitled "Child Development Series for Parents and Educators."

Center for Attitudinal Healing, 19 Main St., Tiburon, Ca. 94920. Support groups for children and families of children facing life-threatening illnesses. Books and audio/video tapes available.

Chief Knight for the Order of the Round Table in America, Mrs. Gudrun Murti, c/o Theosophical Society, P. O. Box 270, Wheaton, Il. 61809. Organization to help children (5 +) become aware of higher principles of life.

Growing Without Schooling, 729 Boylston St., Boston, Ma. 02116. Network of parents who are teaching children at home. Publishes newsletter. Also provides mail order booklist of children's literature, books on learning, tapes, and a few learning tools (e.g. art supplies, metronomes, etc.). Founded and directed by John Holt and his associates.

Hearth Song: A Catalog for Families, 2211 Blucher Valley Rd., Sebastopol, Ca. 95472. Mail order catalog of natural clothes, dolls, crafts, health supplies, children's literature, books on learning, art supplies (e.g. beeswax crayons, high quality water colors). Rudolf Steiner perspective.

The Laughing Man Institute, 740 Adrian Way, San Rafael, Ca. 94903. Attn. children's dept. (415 492-0930). Conducts "Conscious Child-Raising" workshops. Distributes the book "Look at the Sunlight on the Water" (see annotated bibliography).

Mothering Magazine, P. O. Box 8410, Santa Fe, N. M. 87504 (505 984-8116). Quarterly magazine on new age and progressive approaches to birthing, parenting, and education. Frequent articles on Waldorf Education, spiritual aspects of child development, etc.

Our Ultimate Investment, 5615 W. Pico Blvd., Los Angeles, Ca. 90019. "Caressing centers" give older individuals an opportunity to hold and care for babies. Fosters grandparent-grandchild relationship. Laura Huxley, founder.

Parents' Theosophical Research Group, 336 South Pueblo Ave., Ojai, Ca. 93023. Membership includes subscription to quarterly newsletter *Parents Bulletin*. Also publishes *The Theosophical Guide for Parents* (see annotated bibliography).

Rosicrucian Fellowship, 2222 Mission Ave., P. O. Box 713, Oceanside, Ca. 92054. Books for children (*Aquarian Age Stories for Children*), books on astrology and your child, *Rosicrucian Principles of Child Training* (see annotated bibliography).

Vedanta Society Bookshop, 2323 Vallejo St., San Francisco, Ca. 94123. Children's books available by mail order, including life of Ramakrishna, Vivekananda, Indian myths, fables, folktales, history of religions, etc.

St. George Book Service, P. O. Box 225, Spring Valley, N. Y. 10977. Books on Waldorf education available by mail, including *The Waldorf Parenting Handbook.*

Anthroposophic Press, 258 Hungry Hollow Rd., Spring Valley, N.Y. 10977. Books on Rudolf Steiner's theories of child development, Waldorf education, etc.

Psychotherapy

Association for Transpersonal Psychology, P. O. Box 3049, Stanford, Ca. 94305. For professionals and nonprofessionals interested in transpersonal studies. Biannual journal and annual and regional conferences explore developmental issues and childhood education.

Jungian Dreamwork Institute, 1525 J Shattuck Ave., Berkeley, Ca. 94709 (415-540-5500). Conducts periodic Transforming Childhood weekend workshops (for adults). Titles include: "Awakening the Wondrous Child" and "The Soul of the Inner Child."

California Institute of Integral Studies, 755 Ashbury St., San Francisco. Ca. 94117. Opportunity for study at the M.A. and Ph.D. level on the spiritual nature of childhood (title of recent dissertation: "A Psychology of Human Possibility: The Rationale for a Psychospiritual Approach to Child Development"). WASC accredited. Programs in clinical, counseling, and East-West psychology, philosophy, religion, and anthropology.

California Institute of Transpersonal Psychology, 250 Oak Grove Ave., Menlo Park, Ca 94025. Ph.D. program in transpersonal psychology. Opportunity for work on the spiritual dimensions of childhood.

John F. Kennedy University, 12 Altarinda Rd., Orinda, Ca. 94563 (415-254-0200). B.A. and M.A. programs in consciousness studies, transpersonal counseling, parapsychology. Offers periodic course in "The Psychic and Spiritual Life of the Child" and other child development courses embodying a transpersonal approach. Program in Integrative Education offers opportunities for work in transpersonal education.

Hilde Kirsch Children's Center, 10349 W. Pico Blvd., Los Angeles, Ca. 90064 (213-556-1193). Jungian training institute for child therapists and counselors.

Rosebridge Institute, 2910 Camino Diablo, Walnut Creek, Ca., 94596. M.A. and Ph.D. granting institute founded by Dr. Ernest Pecci whose work with the psychic dimensions of childhood schizophrenia and the healing of the wounded "inner child" have been pioneering efforts. Specialization available in Integrative Childhood and Adolescent Psychology.

Saybrook Institute, 1772 Vallejo St., San Francisco, Ca., 94123. Ph.D. degree in psychology. Formerly The Humanistic Psychology Institute. Opportunities for research in psychic/spiritual dimensions of childhood. Contact: Stanley Krippner, Director, Center for Consciousness Studies.

Uniquity, 215 4th St., P. O. Box 6, Galt, Ca. 95632, (209-745-2111). Mail order catalog for resources in education and therapy. Includes sections on play therapy, sand play, and birth/parenting books for kids.

Child Development Research

Brain/Mind Bulletin, P. O. Box 42211, Los Angeles, Ca. 90042. Newsletter. Frequent articles on children and consciousness issues. Published every three weeks.

Child Quest Conference Tapes, Continuum Foundation, P. O. Box 880, Sierra Madre, Ca. 91024 (213-355-4913). Tapes for sale from the Child Quest Conference sponsored by Searchlight Seminars in Walnut Creek, Ca., October, 1978. Topics include psychic sensitivity in children, religious instruction, the child and death, metaphysics of child development, spiritual parenting, and use of fairy tales.

Children's Cancer Research Institute, 2351 Clay Street, Suite 512, San Francisco, Ca. 94115. Artwork available (calendars, greeting cards, etc.) done by children facing catastrophic illness. Help support this facility which is part of Pacific Medical Center. (Family members are allowed to live in the hospital 24 hours a day while the child is undergoing treatment.)

Division of Parapsychology, Box 152, Medical Center, c/o University of Virginia, Charlottesville, Va. 22903 (804-924-2281). Involved in research on children's claimed memories of former lifetimes and other parapsychological issues at the childhood level. Ian Stevenson, M.D., Director of Research.

East-West Bookshop, 1170 El Camino Real, Menlo Park, Ca. 94025 (415-325-5709). One of the largest metaphysical/transpersonal bookstores in the country. Large selection of children's books available by mail order.

Foundation for Mind Research, Box 600, Pomona, N. Y. 10970. Jean Houston, director. Conducts "New Ways of Being Workshops" nationally. Research in human potential.

The Alister Hardy Research Centre, Manchester College, Oxford, OX1 3TD, England. Involved in studying religious experience in childhood. Relationship of art and creativity to spirituality. Edward Robinson, Director.

Latebloomers Educational Consulting Services, P. O. Box 2647, Berkeley, CA 94702. Research on learning potentials. Emphasis on exploring the untapped learning abilities of children and adults who have been labeled "learning disabled" or who have experienced frustration in learning environments. Individual work, workshops for parents and teachers, consulting with schools and industry.

National Association for Gifted Children, 217 Gregory Dr., Hot Springs, Ark. 71901. Publishes *Gifted Child Quarterly* which includes research in creativity, consciousness, and related issues.

Olcott Library and Research Center, P. O. Box 270, Wheaton, Ill. 61089. Maintains a mail-service lending library for a small fee. Publishes list of over 300 books for children and 100 books for parents. Send $1 for each list.

Notes

Chapter 1

1. J. Bronowski, ed., *William Blake: A Selection of Poems and Letters* (Harmondsworth, England: Penguin, 1958), p. 33.
2. Margaret S. Mahler, Fred Pines, and Anni Bergman, *The Psychological Birth of the Human Infant* (New York: Basic Books, 1975), p. 42.
3. Luke 18: 16-17.
4. James Legge, trans., *The Works of Mencius* in *The Chinese Classics* (Vol. II) (Oxford: The Clarendon Press), 1895.
5. Herryman Maurer, trans., *The Way of the Ways: Tao Teh Ching* (Princeton, N. J.: Fellowship in Prayer, 1982), p. 69.
6. Thomas Traherne, Gladys Wade, ed., *The Poetical Works* (New York: Cooper Square Pub. Inc., 1965).
7. William Wordsworth, "Ode: Intimations of Immortality from Recollections of Early Childhood," in Alexander W. Allison et al., eds., *The Norton Anthology of Poetry* (rev. ed.) (New York: W. W. Norton & Company, Inc., 1975), p. 602.
8. E. D. Hirsch, Jr., *Innocence and Experience: An Introduction to Blake* (Chicago: University of Chicago Press, 1964), p. 34.
9. Ernest Schactel, "On memory and childhood amensia," in Toby Talbott, ed., *The World of the Child* (Garden City, N. Y.: Doubleday & Co., Inc., 1967), p. 28.
10. In his commentary on Thomas Traherne's blissful recollections of infancy, D. T. Suzuki noted " . . . we have never forgotten, mythologically speaking, the original abode of innocence; that is to say, even when we are given over to intellection and to the abstract way of thinking, we are always conscious, however dimly, of something left behind and not appearing on the chart of well-schematized analysis. This "something" is no other than the primary experience of reality in its suchness or is-ness, or in its sono-mama ["I Am That I Am"] state of existence." D. T. Suzuki,

Mysticism: Christian and Buddhist (New York: Collier, 1957), p. 80.

11. Rudolf Otto, *The Idea of the Holy* (London: Oxford University Press, 1931).

12. Geoffrey Hodson, *The Miracle of Birth* (Wheaton, Ill.: Theosophical Publishing House, 1981), p. 98.

13. Ken Wilber, *Up From Eden* (Boulder, Co.: Shambhala, 1981), pp. 25-26.

14. Joseph Chilton Pearce, *Magical Child* (New York: Bantam, 1980), p. 25.

15. Hazrat Inayat Khan, *The Sufi Message*, (Vol. III) (London: Barrie and Jenkins, 1971), p. 13.

16. Wordsworth, *The Norton Anthology of Poetry*, p. 602.

17. Freud responded to Romain Rolland's defense of authentic religious feeling by declaring that this "oceanic feeling was nothing but an echo of man's infantile helplessness." Sigmund Freud, "Civilization and Its Discontents," in James Strachey, trans., *The Complete Psychological Works of Sigmund Freud* Vol. XXI (1927-31), (London: The Hogarth Press, 1978), pp. 64-73. Freud's view of the origins of the God concept (that it is a vestige of one's early perceptions of the father) have been revised and updated by Ana-Maria Rizzuto in *The Birth of the Living God* (Chicago: University of Chicago Press, 1979).

Chapter 2

1. J. D. Salinger, "Teddy," in *Nine Stories* (New York: Signet, 1954), p. 138.

2. Marie-Louise von Franz, *Individuation in Fairy Tales*, (Zurich: Spring Publications, 1977), p. 13.

3. Franklin Jones, *The Knee of Listening* (Los Angeles, Ca.: The Ashram, 1972), pp. 9-10.

4. E. D. Starbuck, *The Psychology of Religion* (London: Walter, Scott, 1906), p. 194.

5. Quoted in Ronald Goldman, *Religious Thinking from Childhood to Adolescence* (London: Routledge and Kegan Paul, 1964), p. 4.

6. See Goldman, *Religious Thinking from Childhood to Adolescence*; James W. Fowler, *Stages of Faith: The Psychology of Human Development and the Quest for Meaning* (San Francisco: Harper & Row, 1981); and David Elkind, Religious Development, in *The Child's Reality: Three Developmental Themes* (Hillsdale, N.J.: Lawrence Erlbaum Assoc. Pub., 1978).

7. Augusta Theodosia Drane, *The History of St. Catherine of Siena*, Vol. 1 (2nd ed.), (London: Burns and Oates Ltd., 1880), pp. 12-13.

8. A. Gilchrist, *Life of William Blake*, (Totowa, N. J.: Rowman & Littlefield, 1973), p. 7.

9. John Lilly, *Center of the Cyclone*, (New York: Bantam, 1973), pp. 12-13.

10. Annette Hollander, *How to Help Your Child Have a Spiritual Life*, (New York: Bantam, 1982), p. 21.

11. Personal communication, January 2, 1985.

12. John Lilly, *Center of the Cyclone*, p. 12-13.

13. Abraham Maslow, *Toward a Psychology of Being* (New York: D. Van Nostrand Co. Inc., 1962), p. 67.

14. S. Nikhilananda, trans., *The Gospel of Sri Ramakrishna* (abridged ed.), (New York: Ramakrishna-Vivekananda Center, 1970), pp. 3-4.

15. K. R. S. Iyengar, *On the Mother: The Chronicle of a Manifestation and Ministry* (Pondicherry, India: Sri Aurobindo International Centre of Education, 1952), p. 4.

16. Jean Houston, *The Possible Human* (Los Angeles: J. P. Tarcher, 1982), p. 186.

17. Edward Robinson, *The Original Vision: A Study of the Religious Experience of Childhood*, (Oxford: The Religious Experience Research Unit, Manchester College, 1977), pp. 32-3.

18. William James, *Varieties of Religious Experience*, (New York: The New American Library [1902], 1958), p. 305.

19. Ibid., p. 304.

20. Richard Maurice Bucke, *Cosmic Consciousness* (New York: E. P. Dutton, [1901] 1966), p. 346.

21. Raymond A. Moody, *Life After Life* (Atlanta, Ga.: Mockingbird, 1975). See also Kenneth Ring, *Life at Death: A Scientific Investigation of the Near-Death Experience*, (New York: Coward, McCann & Geoghegan, 1980).

22. M. Morse, "A near-death experience in a 7-year-old child." *American Journal of Diseases of Children*, 137, 1983, 959-961.

23. Quoted in Nancy Evans Bush, "The near-death experience in children: Shades of the Prison-House Reopening." *ANABIOSIS-The Journal for Near-Death Studies* Vol. 3, Number 2, December 1983, pp. 3-4.

24. Paramahansa Yogananda, *Autobiography of a Yogi* (Los Angeles: Self-Realization Fellowship, 1969), p. 10.

25. J. G. Neihardt, *Black Elk Speaks* (Lincoln: University of Nebraska Press, 1961), p. 43.

26. Quoted in Francis Wickes, *The Inner World of Childhood* (New York: Mentor, 1963), p. 83.

27. Psalms 8:2.

28. C. G. Jung, "Psychic Conflicts in a Child" in R. F. C. Hull, trans., *The Development of Personality* (Princeton, N. J.: Princeton University Press, 1954), pp. 9-10.

29. Annette Hollander, *How to Help Your Child Have a Spiritual Life*, pp. 27-28.

30. Elisabeth Kübler-Ross, *On Children and Death*, (New York: Macmillan, 1983), pp. 221-224.

31. Violet Madge, *Children in Search of Meaning* (New York: Morehouse-Barlow Co., 1966), p. 96.

32. Rhoda Kellogg, *Analyzing Children's Art* (Palo Alto, Ca.: Mayfield, 1970).

33. Michael Fordham, *Children as Individuals* (New York: Putnam, 1969).

34. Edward Robinson, *The Original Vision*, p. 112.

35. Ibid., pp. 27-28.

36. Ibid., p. 115.

37. See for example, Margaret Anderson and Rhea White, "A Survey of Work on ESP and Teacher-Pupil Attitudes," *Journal of Parapsychology*, 22, 4, December 1958, pp. 246-268; and R. L. Van de Castle, "A review of ESP tests carried out in the classroom," *International Journal of Parapsychology*, 1, 2, 1959, 84-99.

38. Bethold Schwartz, *Parent-Child Telepathy: A Study of the Telepathy of Everyday Life*, (New York: Garrett Publications, 1971), p. 53.

39. Jan Ehrenwald, "Parent-child symbiosis: Cradle of ESP" in *The ESP Experience A Psychiatric validation*, (New York: Basic Books, 1978).

40. Jamuna Prasad and Ian Stevenson, "A survey of spontaneous psychical experiences in school children in Uttar Pradesh, India." *International Journal of Parapsychology*, 10:3, Autumn, 1968, 241-261, p. 250.

41. Ibid., p. 251.

42. Elisabeth Kübler-Ross, *On Children and Death*, pp. 131-134.

43. J. R. Musso, "ESP experiments with primary school children." *Journal of Parapsychology*, 29, 1965, 115-121.

44. James Peterson, "Some profiles of non-ordinary perception of children." Unpublished Master's Thesis, University of California, Berkeley, Ca., 1974.

45. James Peterson, "Extrasensory abilities of children: An ignored reality?" *Learning*, December 1975, 11-14.

46. James Peterson, "Some profiles of non-ordinary perception of children," pp. 71-72. The names of the children have been changed.

47. See Chapter Five for a discussion of this "etheric" level of reality, described in metaphysical terms.

48. Matthew Manning, *The Link*, (New York: Holt, Rinehart & Winston, 1975).

49. Joseph Chilton Pearce, *Magical Child*, p. 190.

50. Jean Piaget, quoted in Pearce, *Magical Child*, p. 182.

51. See Jan Ehrenwald, "Parent-child symbiosis and the revolt of the poltergeist." In *The ESP Experience: A psychiatric validation.*

Chapter 3

1. Helen Wambach, *Life Before Life* (New York: Bantam, 1979), p. 186.

2. David Chamberlain, *Consciousness at Birth: A Review of the Empirical Evidence* (San Diego: Chamberlain Communications, 1983), p. 34.

3. Ibid., p. 34.

4. There is an increasing awareness in medical science that *in utero* awareness is possible. Chamberlain reviews some of the evidence for this in *Consciousness at Birth: A Review of the Empirical Evidence*. See also Thomas Verny, *The Secret Life of the Unborn Child* (New York: Delta, 1981). However, most of this research still has far to go to match the suggestion that infants may possess an adult-like component in their earliest consciousness. At best the great part of this research tends to support the idea that rudimentary forms of perception and learning are possible in the womb.

5. " . . . although the myelin sheath is not necessary for conduction of action potentials [electrical activity in the brain], relative rates of myelinization in different areas of the brain can serve as a rough measure of the sequence in which various components of the nervous system approach adult levels of functional effectiveness." Gordon W. Bronson, "Structure, status, and characteristics of the nervous system at birth," in Peter Stratton ed., *Psychobiology of the Human Newborn* (New York: John Wiley & Sons Ltd., 1982), p. 102.

6. Chamberlain's research does not "prove" the existence of an adult-like consciousness in infancy. There are other possible explanations including mother-child collusion, adult mental telepathy and mother-child symbiosis (the primitive psychological unity or "fusion" that was described in Chapter One). However, Chamberlain's research becomes suggestive when lined up in Chapter Two as

well as when compared to other regression research conducted over the past twenty years. See for example Helen Wambach, *Life Before Life* (New York: Bantam, 1979) and Stanislav Grof, *Realms of the Human Unconscious* (New York: Viking, 1975) for even more powerful and sophisticated accounts of pre-birth and birth memories.

7. The first three forces are psychodynamic (Freudian), behavioral, and humanistic. For a good collection of writings applying these world views (as well as the transpersonal world view) to education, see Thomas B. Roberts, *Four Psychologies Applied to Education: Freudian, Behavioral, Humanistic, Transpersonal* (New York: John Wiley & Sons, 1975).

8. Anthony J. Sutich, "Some considerations regarding transpersonal psychology," *Journal of Transpersonal Psychology*, 1, 1969, 16. I will be using the word "transpersonal" in a more limited sense in Chapter Eight. However, where it appears elsewhere in the book I will generally be using it to designate the professional movement or the more general definition given by Sutich.

9. C. G. Jung, *Two Essays in Analytical Psychology* in *Collected Works*, Vol. 7 (New York: Pantheon, 1953), pp. 96, 131, 142, 270. It should be noted that the first individual to use the word *transpersonal* in English was Dane Rudhyar in the 1920s or 1930s. His discussion of the term can be found in *Rhythm of Wholeness* (Wheaton, Ill.: Theosophical Publishing House, 1983).

10. A good historical description of the evolution of the transpersonal psychology movement is found in Anthony J. Sutich, "The emergence of the transpersonal orientation: A personal account." *The Journal of Transpersonal Psychology*, 8, 1976, 5-19.

11. For an excellent discussion of the Jungian concepts of ego and Self and their relationship to similar terms in other psychological schools, see J. W. T. Redfearn, "Ego and self: Terminology," *Journal of Analytical Psychology*, 23, 1983, 91-106.

12. See for example, C. G. Jung, "Child Development and Education," in *Psychology and Education* (Princeton, N. J.: Princeton University Press, 1974). This intimate link between parent and child unconscious can help to explain many of the telepathic, clairvoyant and psychokinetic experiences described in Chapter Two. For a neo-Jungian interpretation, see Erich Neumann, *The Child: Structure and Dynamics of the Nascent Personality* (New York: Harper & Row, 1973).

13. C. G. Jung, *Memories, Dreams, Reflections* (New York: Vintage, 1963), pp. 11-12.

14. Ibid., p. 15.

15. C. G. Jung, "The stages of life," in Joseph Campbell, ed., *The Portable Jung* (New York: Viking, 1971).

16. Frances Wickes, *The Inner World of Childhood* (New York: Mentor, 1966), p. ix.

17. Dora M. Kalff, *Sandplay: A Psychotherapeutic Approach to the Psyche* (Santa Monica, CA: Sigo Press, 1980), p. 65.

18. From Roberto Assagioli, *Psychosynthesis* (New York: Viking, 1965), p. 17. Reprinted by permission of the Berkshire Center for Psychosynthesis, Inc.

19. Ibid., p. 17-18.

20. The "higher self" should not be equated with Jung's Self although there are some similarities between them. For a discussion of the differences, see Roberto Assagioli, "Jung and psychosynthesis" (New York: Psychosynthesis Research Foundation, 1967) pamphlet.

21. Roberto Assagioli, "The education of gifted and supergifted children" (New York: Psychosynthesis Research Foundation, 1960) pamphlet, p. 8.

22. Jack Canfield and Paula Klimek, "Education in the new age," *New Age*, February 1978, p. 32.

23. Ibid., pp. 32-33.

24. John Welwood, "Meditation and the unconscious: A new perspective," in John Welwood, ed., *The Meeting of the Ways* (New York: Shocken, 1979), p. 161.

25. Ibid., pp. 161-162.

26. Ibid., p. 166.

27. John Welwood, "On psychological space," *The Journal of Transpersonal Psychology*, 9:2, 1977, 109. (Cf. Chapter 1, n. 10 of this book.).

28. Taken from Ken Wilber, *The Atman Project* (Wheaton, Ill.: Theosophical Publishing House, 1980), p. 50.

29. A discussion of the other four kinds of unconscious is beyond the scope of this book. See Ken Wilber, "Development, meditation, and the unconscious." in *Eye to Eye: The Quest for the New Paradigm* (Garden City, New York: Anchor/Doubleday, 1983).

30. Wilber, "The Pre/Trans Fallacy," *Revision*, 3:2, 1980, p. 61. Also in *Eye to Eye*.

31. Wilber, *The Atman Project*, p. 91.

32. These of course may be equivalent ways of talking about the same thing, using different terminology and conceptual frameworks.

Chapter Four

1. Hazrat Inayat Khan, "The Education of the Baby," in *The Sufi Message*, Vol. III, (London: Barrie and Jenkins, 1960), pp. 34-35.

2. Otto Rank, "The myth of the birth of the hero: A psychological interpretation of mythology." in *The Myth of the Birth of the Hero and Other Writings* (New York: Vintage, 1964, [Originally published in 1914]), p. 65.

3. The following accounts have been adapted from Rank, *The Myth of the Birth of the Hero and Other Writings.*

4. Joseph Campbell, *The Mythic Image* (Princeton, N.J.: Princeton University Press, 1974), p. 44.

5. Rank, *The Myth of the Birth of the Hero and Other Writings,* p. 71.

6. R. D. Laing, *The Facts of Life* (New York: Pantheon, 1976), pp. 36-37.

7. The current debate between creationists and evolutionists on the subject of human origins will probably remain clouded until this dual line of development (down from the spirit/up from the body) is applied to mankind as a whole. Each side holds a piece of the puzzle.

8. Ken Wilber in *Up From Eden* has attempted to resolve this dual aspect of human origins by collapsing the spiritual into the material. Eden in his view was not transpersonal at all, but rather a state of "pre-personal ignorance." According to Wilber, civilization has developed from very primitive levels of consciousness to increasing levels of sophistication and articulation. Only after a long period of development does civilization reach into spiritual or transpersonal regions of accomplishment and discovery. Fortunately Wilber's viewpoint has not prevented a group of dedicated anthropologists from forming an Association of Transpersonal Anthropology which believes that authentically transpersonal experiences are present in the earliest stages of collective human development. Their journal *Phoenix* is available by writing: Association for Transpersonal Anthropology Intl., 2001 Tibbits Ave., Troy, N.Y. 12180.

9. H. P. Blavatsky, *An Abridgement of the Secret Doctrine* (London: The Theosophical Publishing House, 1966), p. 178.

10. Genesis 2-3.

11. Thomas J. Hopkins, *The Hindu Religious Tradition* (Encino, Ca.: Dickenson Pub. Co. Inc., 1971), p. 101.

12. Richard Cavendish, *Man, Myth and Magic* (London: Cavendish, 1983), p. 2851.

13. Ibid.

14. See for example, Roy Stemman, *Atlantis and the Lost Lands* (Garden City, N. Y.: Doubleday and Company, Inc., 1977).

15. See for example, Charles Berlitz, *Mysteries from Forgotten*

Worlds (Garden City, New York: Doubleday & Company, Inc., 1972).

16. Edwin Bernbaum, *The Way to Shambhala* (Garden City, N.Y.: Anchor/Doubleday, 1980), p. 250.

17. Ibid.

18. Clifford John Williams, "The Lord's song in a strange land" in *The Spiritual Hunger of the Modern Child: A Series of Ten Lectures* (Charles Town W. Va.: Claymont Communications, 1984), p. 32.

19. See Neumann's *The Great Mother* (Princeton, N. J.: Princeton University Press, 1972) for a detailed description of this archetype.

20. See especially the chapters "The slaying of the mother" and "The slaying of the father" in Erich Neumann, *The Origins and History of Consciousness* (Princeton, N. J.: Princeton University Press, 1971), pp. 153-194.

21. Bernbaum, *The Way to Shambhala*, p. 263.

22. Joseph Campbell, *The Hero with a Thousand Faces* (Princeton, N. J.: Princeton University Press, 1973), pp. 71-72.

23. Wickes, *The Inner World of Childhood*, pp. 257-258.

Chapter Five

1. Quoted in Narayan Prasad, "Sparks of Psychic Fire." in *Education for a New Life* (Pondicherry, India: Sri Aurobindo Ashram Press, 1976), p. 10.

2. Ian Stevenson, *Cases of the Reincarnation Type, Volume IV, Twelve Cases in Thailand and Burma* (Charlottesville, VA.: University Press of Virginia, 1983), pp. 12-13.

3. Ian Stevenson, "The explanatory value of the idea of reincarnation," *The Journal of Nervous and Mental Disease*, 164, 1977, 307-308.

4. In addition to the sources cited above, Stevenson's work includes (but is not limited to) the following: Ian Stevenson, *Twenty Cases Suggestive of Reincarnation* (New York: American Society for Psychical Research, 1966); Ian Stevenson, *Cases of the Reincarnation Type: Volume I, Ten Cases in India* (Charlottesville, Va.: University Press of Virigina, 1975); Ian Stevenson, *Cases of the Reincarnation Type: Volume II: Ten Cases in Sri Lanka* (Charlottesville, Va.: University Press of Virginia, 1977); Ian Stevenson, *Cases of the Reincarnation Type: Volume III, Twelve Cases in Lebanon and Turkey* (Charlottesville, Va.: University Press of Virginia, 1980); and Ian Stevenson, "American children who claim

to remember previous lives," *The Journal of Nervous and Mental Disease*, 171, 1983, 742-748.

5. Huston Smith, *Forgotten Truth* (New York: Harper and Row, 1967), p. 62.

6. Smith, *Forgotten Truth*, p. 74.

7. Rupert Sheldrake, *A New Science of Life: The Hypothesis of Formative Causation* (Los Angeles: J. P. Tarcher, Inc., 1981), p. 72. Morphogenetic field theory is applicable not only to the etheric field but to all other fields in esoteric psychology since, according to Sheldrake, "morphogenetic fields . . . are essentially hierarchical in their organization." (p. 74). It is interesting to note that while Joseph Chilton Pearce (and Ken Wilber) regard earth/mother as the primary matrix, M-field theory and esoteric psychology see physical matter as being essentially molded by higher formative matrices. Thus, once again, we see the distinction between "body up" and "spirit down" approaches to living systems and the psyche.

8. See Dolores Krieger, *Therapeutic Touch* (Englewood Cliffs, N.J.: Prentice Hall, 1979).

9. For a fascinating "field guide" to this world, see C. W. Leadbeater, *The Astral Plane* (Adyar, India: The Theosophical Publishing House, 1973).

10. See Annie Besant and C. W. Leadbeater, *Thought-Forms* (Wheaton, Ill.: Quest Books, 1969).

11. I. K. Taimni, *A Way to Self-Discovery* (Wheaton, Ill.: Quest Books, 1970), pp. 134-135.

12. Taken from Thomas Armstrong, "Transpersonal Experience in Childhood," *Journal of Transpersonal Psychology*, 1984, 16:2, p. 215. Used with permission of the Transpersonal Institute ©. The levels of personality development are adapted from Rudolf Steiner, *The Education of the Child in the Light of Anthroposophy* (London: Rudolf Steiner Press, 1965).

13. See Rudolf Steiner, *A Modern Art of Education* (London: Rudolf Steiner Press, 1972), p. 80.

14. Laurence J. Bendit and Phoebe D. Bendit, *The Etheric Body of Man* (Wheaton, Ill.: Quest Books, 1977), p. 57. As mentioned in the text, the chakras are centers of consciousness through which the energies of the different fields of the psyche are integrated and synthesized. There are said to be seven chakras according to Indian metaphysics. The lowest or first chakra is situated at the base of the spine and regulates the survival instinct in a human being. The second chakra is located near the genitals and is concerned with sexual energy. The third chakra is situated near the solar plexus and relates to power and aggression. The fourth chakra is in the heart center

and is the source of compassionate and loving energy. The fifth chakra is located in the throat area and is said to amplify the longing and seeking for God or higher truth. The sixth chakra is frequently referred to as the "third eye" and is situated between and slightly above the eyes. It is the vehicle of inner wisdom. Finally, the seventh chakra is located at the crown of the head and is the "thousand-petaled lotus" which connects the individual to infinity. The chakras function at varying levels of activity depending on the relative development of each individual. For more information, see C. W. Leadbeater, *The Chakras* (Wheaton, Ill.: Quest Books, 1977).

15. Bendit and Bendit, *The Etheric Body of Man*, p. 59.

16. See Joseph Head and S. L. Cranton, *Reincarnation: An East-West Anthology* (Wheaton, Ill.: The Theosophical Publishing House, 1981).

17. W. Y. Evans-Wentz, trans. *The Tibetan Book of the Dead* (Oxford: Oxford University Press, 1960).

Chapter Six

1. Brown, Joseph Epes, ed., *The Sacred Pipe, Black Elk's Account of the Seven Rites of the Oglala Sioux* (Norman, OK: Univ. of Oklahoma Press, 1953). Quoted in *Parabola*, 4:3, 1979, p. 70.

2. C. G. Jung, "The psychology of the child archetype," in *The Archetypes and the Collective Unconscious, The Collected Works of C. G. Jung* Vol. 9, Part 1 (New York: Pantheon, 1959), p. 179.

3. Joseph Campbell, *The Mythic Image* (Princeton, N. J.: Princeton University Press, 1974), p. 287.

4. C. Kerenyi, "The primordial child in primordial times" in *Essays on a Science of Mythology* (New York: Harper and Row, 1963).

5. G. W. Meek, ed., *Healers and the Healing Process* (Wheaton, Ill.: The Theosophical Publishing House, 1977), p. 29.

6. Bendit and Bendit, *The Etheric Body of Man*.

7. See Hodson, *The Miracle of Birth* for a description of how the mother's positive thoughts and spiritual aspirations are meditated by angelic forces and used to nurture the growing fetus.

8. Joan Halifax, *Shaman: The Wounded Healer*, (New York: Crossroads, 1982), p. 11.

9. Ninian Smart, *The Religious Experience of Mankind* (New York: Charles Scribner's Sons, 1976), pp. 375-76.

10. Personal communication, October, 1983.

11. Joseph Chilton Pearce, *Magical Child*, pp. 181-182.

12. J. Harrison, quoted in Michael Fordham, *Children as Individuals* (New York: G. P. Putnam's Sons, 1969), p. 32.

13. Peter Morley and Roy Wallis, eds., *Culture and Curing: Anthropological Perspectives on Traditional Medical Beliefs and Practices* (London: Peter Owne, 1978), p. 42.

14. Joseph Campbell, *Myths to Live By* (New York: Bantam, 1972), p. 210.

15. Lyall Watson, *Lifetide: The Biology of Consciousness* (New York: Simon and Schuster, 1980).

16. A recent article calls into question the validity of this story. See Maureen O'Hara, "Of Myths and Monkeys: A Critical Look at a Theory of Critical Mass," *Journal of Humanistic Psychology*, 25:1, 1985, 61-78. O'Hara's arguments do not affect us here, however, for we are not concerned so much with critical mass as with the fact that these changes, however transmitted, originated through the genius of an infant.

17. Although children are powerfully influenced by the structures of the culture as they come "up from the body," they also seem to bring something unique or original into that interchange as well, something that is arguably a product of their journey "down from the spirit."

18. Kornei Chukovsky, *From Two to Five* (Berkeley: University of California Press, 1963).

19. Lewis Thomas, *Late Night Thoughts on Listening to Mahler's Ninth Symphony* (New York: Viking, 1983), pp. 60-61.

20. Derek Bickerton, "Creole languages." *Scientific American*, 249, July 1982, pp. 116-22.

21. John M. Chernoff, "Music-making children of Africa." *Natural History*, 88, 1979, 75.

22. Jeremy Bernstein, *Einstein*, (Harmondsworth, G. B.: Penguin, 1973), p. 16.

23. John B. Schaffer and David M. Glinsky, *Models of Group Therapy and Sensitivity Training* (Englewood Cliffs, N. J.: Prentice-Hall, 1974), pp. 108-109.

24. Erich Neumann, "Leonardo Da Vinci and the mother archetype." *Art and the Creative Unconscious* (Princeton, N. J.: Princeton University Press, [1959], 1974).

25. Quoted in Marshall McLuhan and Quentin Fiore, *The Medium is the Message* (New York: Bantam, 1967), p. 93.

26. Ashley Montagu, *Growing Young* (New York: McGraw-Hill, 1983).

27. Dan Kiley, *The Peter Pan Syndrome: Men Who Have Never Grown Up* (New York: Avon, 1983).

28. Marie-Louise von Franz, *Puer Aeternus* (Santa Monica, Ca.: Sigo Press, 1970).

29. Ibid., p. 13.
30. Wilhelm Reich, *Character Analysis* (New York: Orgone Institute Press, 1949).
31. Arthur Janov, *The Primal Scream* (New York: G. P. Putnam's Sons, 1980).
32. Bob Hoffman, *No One is to Blame: Getting a Loving Divorce from Mom and Dad* (Palo Alto, Ca.: Science and Behavior Books, Inc., 1979).
33. Muriel James and Dorothy Jongeward, *Born to Win* (Reading, Mass.: Addison-Wesley Inc., 1976).
34. James Vargiu, "Subpersonalities." *Synthesis*, 1:1, 1974, WB9-WB47.
35. C. G. Jung, *Memories, Dreams, Reflections* (New York: Vintage, 1963), p. 174.
36. One needs to acknowledge that many religious cults while appealing to the child-like within their devotees, have child-ish roots which seek to suck their spiritual aspirants into destructive patterns of dependency. The People's Temple of Jim Jones is a good example. See Ken Wilber, *A Sociable God: Toward a New Understanding of Religion* (Boulder, Co.: Shambhala, 1984) for an excellent discussion of this problem.
37. M. G. Eshelman and B. B. Bert, "Threes and eighty-threes: growing together." *Day Care and Early Education*, Spring 1981, 7-10.
38. "Back from world peace mission," *San Francisco Sunday Examiner and Chronicle*, Jan. 15, 1984, B2.
39. "Children arrive for peace prizes." *San Francisco Chronicle*, May 29, 1984.
40. Gail Pierce, "Children's gardens." *New Age*, October, 1983.
41. C. G. Jung, "The Psychology of the child archetype," p. 164. Italics are mine.

Chapter Seven

1. From "Two Essays on Analytical Psychology," in Joseph Campbell, ed., *The Portable Jung* (New York: Viking, 1971), p. 91.
2. William James, *Principles of Psychology* (Cambridge, Mass: Harvard University Press, 1983), p. 462.
3. C. G. Jung, "The stages of life," R. F. C. Hull, trans., *The Collected Works of C. G. Jung*, Vol. 8. (New York: Pantheon, 1930, 1960), p. 390.
4. Stanislav Grof, *Realms of the Human Unconscious* (New York: Dutton, 1976), p. 45.
5. See for example Ken Wilber, *The Spectrum of Consciousness*

(Wheaton, Il: Theosophical Publishing House, 1977) and Ken Wilber, *No Boundary* (Boulder, CO: Shambhala, 1981).

6. Ken Wilber, *The Atman Project* (Wheaton, Il: Theosophical Publishing House, 1980), p. x.

7. Ken Wilber, "The pre/trans fallacy," *Re-Vision*, 3:2, 1980, 51-72.

8. Ken Wilber, *The Atman Project*, p. 90.

9. Ibid., pp. 160-176.

10. Abraham Maslow, *The Farther Reaches of Human Nature* (New York: Viking, 1971), p. 256.

11. In India, the image of the child Krishna is worshipped by millions as a manifestation of perfection. Also, note the legend concerning The Buddha's wisdom in infancy in Kerenyi.

12. Chogyam Trungpa, *Born in Tibet* (Baltimore, MD: Penguin, 1971). See also, Lobsang Lhalungpa, "The Child Incarnate" in *Parabola*, 4, 1979.

13. C. G. Jung, "Psychological aspects of the mother archetype" R. F. C. Hull, trans., *The Collected Works of C. G. Jung*, p. 77.

14. See Thomas Verny, *The Secret Life of the Unborn Child* (ch. 3, n. 4), and David Chamberlain, *Consciousness at Birth: A Review of the Empirical Evidence* (ch. 3, n. 2).

15. Taken from Thomas Armstrong, "Transpersonal Experience in Childhood," *Journal of Transpersonal Psychology*, 16:2, 1984, p. 222. Used by permission of The Transpersonal Institute ©.

16. Wilber's use of the three-fold distinction—pre-personal, personal, and transpersonal—is taken from R. W. Wescott, *The Divine Animal* (New York: Funk and Wagnalls, 1969), a portion of which is included as "States of consciousness" in J. White, ed., *The Highest State of Consciousness* (New York: Anchor, 1972).

17. This scheme does not require a belief in reincarnation to account for the broader developmental spectrum. This larger spectrum could also very well describe an individual's alignment or openness to his or her own deeper Self without reference to any previous existence.

18. By the same token, this does not mean that very "young" souls are absolutely barred from transpersonal experience. Mystical lore does include stories of neophytes just beginning their long journey toward God being graced with transcendental awakening, essentially skipping much of the middle ground in the process.

19. John H. Flavell, *The Developmental Psychology of Jean Piaget* (New York: D. Van Nostrand Company, 1963), pp. 22-23.

20. Chamberlain, *Consciousness at Birth* and Verny, *The Secret Life of the Unborn Child*.

21. Neumann, *The Origins and History of Consciousness*, p. 18.

22. Ibid., pp. 22-23.

23. Ibid., p. 23. Interestingly, Wilber has made use of this quotation in *The Atman Project* (p. 100) as an indication that *atman* is present from the very beginning of human development. However, Wilber insists that the soul must identify with every subsequent stage of the atman project (each of which is only a partial answer to the desire of the soul for self-knowledge) before attaining enlightenment or even true transpersonal knowledge. I would claim that this light that shines so brightly from the very beginning constitutes authentic transpersonal knowledge in its own right, regardless of what the soul must face on the road ahead.

24. Part of the problem here is the way in which Wilber equates transpersonal levels with personal and prepersonal levels on a structurally equal basis, as if one could simply tack on the transpersonal to the prepersonal and personal stages just like one attaches plastic connectors in a set of lego toys ("If we take all these higher stages and add them to the lower and middle stages/levels . . . we would then arrive at a fairly well-balanced and comprehensive model of the spectrum of consciousness," *The Atman Project*, p. 3). This, I believe, is what Wilber calls a "category error." Transpersonal structures, constituting the deepest components of the psyche, cannot merely be represented as the "latter realms" of development. They are *trans*personal not *post*personal structures. As such, they go beyond the developing structures of personality (prepersonal and personal). They are not simply what comes after these lower levels. At the same time, the transpersonal levels underlie and even interpenetrate the prepersonal and personal in complex ways. Wilber has compared the arrangement of levels in the psyche with geological stratification: "Very like the geological formation of the earth, psychological development proceeds, stratum by stratum, level by level, stage by stage, with each successive level superimposed upon its predecessor in such a way that it includes but transcends it." This may be true in theory, but not when it comes to the complexities of individual human development. As Neumann correctly noted: "We must . . . emphasize that "stage" refers to a structural layer and not to any historical epoch. In individual development and perhaps also in that of the collective, these layers do not lie on top of one another in an orderly arrangememt, but, as in the geological stratification of the earth, early layers may be pushed to the top and late layers to the bottom." (*The Origins and History of Consciousness*, pp. 42-43).

Chapter Eight

1. Quoted in Walter De La Mare, *Early One Morning in the Spring* (New York: Macmillan Company, 1935), p. 193.

2. Samuel Young, *Psychic Children* (Garden City, N. Y.: Doubleday, 1977), pp. 115-116.

3. C. G. Jung, "The self." R. F. C. Hull, trans., *The Collected Works of C. G. Jung* 9:2, 1959, 173.

4. Pearce, *Magical Child*. (ch. 1 n. 14).

5. E. Bruce Taub-Bynum, *The Family Unconscious* (Wheaton, Ill.: Theosophical Publishing House, 1984).

6. C. G. Jung, "Child Development and Education," R. F. C. Hull, trans., *Psychology and Education* (Princeton, N. J.: Princeton University Press, 1974).

7. R. D. Laing, *The Politics of the Family and Other Essays* (New York: Vintage, 1972).

8. The work of Joseph Chilton Pearce is especially good in showing how this process takes place in the life of the child. See *Exploring the Crack in the Cosmic Egg* (New York: Julian Press, 1974) and *Magical Child*.

9. It seems likely that if society allowed non-ordinary experiences to filter through its cultural fabric, then this "personal" category would need to be described in very different terms (e.g. it might be harder to make the kind of distinctions I have made between categories). Henry Stack Sullivan noted: "The origin of the self-system can be said to rest on the irrational character of culture. Were it not for the fact that a great many prescribed ways of doing things have to be lived up to, in order that one shall maintain . . . relations, . . . then, for all I know, there would not be evolved, in the course of becoming a person, anything like the sort of self-system that we always encounter." (quoted in Pearce, *Exploring the Crack in the Cosmic Egg*, p. 5).

10. For a comprehensive cross-cultural inventory of the many kinds of knowledge that are transmitted from one generation to the next (and the ways in which that knowledge is transmitted), see Jules Henry, *On Education* (New York: Random House, 1966).

11. Ernest Hilgard, "Imaginary Companions in Childhood." *Personality and Hypnosis* (Chicago: The University of Chicago Press, 1970).

12. J. Louise Despert, *Schizophrenia in Children* (New York: Brunner/Mazel Publishers, 1968), p. 13.

13. See for example, Katherine Briggs, *An Encyclopedia of Fairies: Hobgoblins, Brownies, Bogies and Other Supernatural Creatures* (New York: Random House, 1976); and Geoffrey Hodson, *Fairies at Work and at Play* (Wheaton, IL.: The Theosophical Publishing House, 1982).

14. James Peterson, "Some profiles of non-ordinary perception of children," p. 85. The names of the child and "companion" have been changed.

15. Charles Cayce, "Parapsychology of Children," (cassette), Child Quest Conference, Searchlight Seminars, Walnut Creek, Ca., October, 1978.

16. Wickes, *The Inner World of Childhood*, pp. 156-157.

17. Hilgard, "Imaginary Companions in Childhood."

18. Edith Cobb, *The Ecology of Imagination in Childhood* (New York: Columbia University Press, 1977), pp. 81-82.

19. Samuel Young, *Psychic Children*, pp. 116-117.

20. Ibid., p. 117.

21. Ibid., p. 117-118.

22. Ibid., p. 114.

23. Ibid.

24. At the same time it should be recognized that here also, as with other levels and stages of development, there are experiences that seem to share elements of both subpersonal and suprapersonal categories. As we shall see in Chapter 10, so much of the child's experience is paradoxically of the earth and the spirit simultaneously. So it continues to be wise to let these categories remain general distinctions without laying down any hard and fast rules about them.

25. Wickes, *The Inner World of Childhood*, p. 192.

26. Ibid.

27. "The Soul that rises with us, our life's Star/Hath had elsewhere its setting." William Wordsworth, "Ode: Intimations of Immortality . . . " in *Norton Anthology of Poetry*, p. 602.

Chapter Nine

1. Message to an Indian Montessori School, 1942.

2. George Arundale, *The Bedrock of Education* (Adyar, India: Theosophical Publishing House, 1924), p. 26.

3. Kahlil Gibran, *The Prophet* (New York: Alfred A. Knopf, 1964), p. 17.

4. Hazrat Inayat Khan, *The Sufi Message*, Vol. III, p. 28.

5. Rudolf Steiner, *The Kingdom of Childhood*, (London: Rudolf Steiner Press, 1982), p. 20.

6. Quoted in Annette Hollander, *How to Help Your Child Have a Spiritual Life*, p. 27.

7. Ibid., p. 21.

8. Charles Cayce, "How to work with children with psychic

sensitivity," (cassette), Child Quest Conference, Searchlight Seminars, Walnut Creek, Ca., October, 1978.

9. Panel Discussion, "The world of the psychic child," (cassette), Child Quest Conference, Searchlight Seminars, Walnut Creek, Ca., October, 1978.

10. Referring to teachers and education, Steiner said: "Now it always fills me with horror to see a teacher standing in his class with a book in his hand teaching out of the book . . . . The child does not appear to notice this with his upper consciousness, it is true; but if you are aware of these things then you will see that the children have subconscious wisdom and say to themselves: He does not himself know what I am supposed to be learning. Why should I learn what he does not know?" (*The Kingdom of Childhood*, p. 68). This does not mean that you should not read to your child. There are many wonderful and imaginative story books, poems, novels and dramas that are written to be shared in this way. The point I think Steiner is making here is that a teacher or parent should not use a book as a substitute for real inner knowledge.

11. Cayce, "How to work with children with psychic sensitivity," (cassette). Cayce does feel that groups can be useful and supportive to psychic children if the groups are sensitively developed.

12. C. G. Jung, "Analytical psychology and education," in R. F. C. Hull trans., *Psychology and Education* (Princeton, N. J.: Princeton University Press, 1974).

13. The best discussions that I have ever seen on both the positive and negative experiences of childhood religious instruction are contained in Rev. James Diamond's seminar "The Sunday school anomaly: Providing children with appropriate religious education," (cassette), Child Quest Conference, Searchlight Seminars, Walnut Creek, Ca., October, 1978; and in Annette Hollander, *How to Help Your Child Have a Spiritual Life* (ch. 2 n. 10).

14. Erik Erikson, *Childhood and Society* (New York: W. W. Norton, 1963), p. 251.

15. I need to temper my criticism of guided imagery and meditations by saying that under certain circumstances their use is warranted. They have proven to be valuable in helping children learn academic skills, such as reading, where other methods have failed (see for example, Barbara Meister Vitale, *Unicorns are Real: A Right-Brained Approach to Learning* (Rolling Hills, Ca.: Jalmar, 1982). Likewise they can be useful in work with children with emotional or behavioral problems. However, these activities need to be self-empowering, used in conjunction with other activities, and meaningfully connected to the child's needs and interests.

16. Hazrat Inayat Khan, *The Sufi Message*, Vol. III, pp. 76-77.

17. Edith Sullwold, "Treatment of Children in Analytical Psychology," in Murray Stein, ed., *Jungian Analysis* (Boulder, Colo.: Shambhala, 1984), p. 240.

18. Philip Zaleski, "The New Age Interview: Elisabeth Kübler-Ross." *New Age*, November 1984, p. 41.

19. Ernest Pecci, "Psychic dimensions of autism and schizophrenia in children," (cassette), Child Quest Conference, Searchlight Seminars, Walnut Creek, Ca., October, 1978.

20. An exception to this is Earl Ogletree's "Intellectual Growth in Children and the Theory of 'Bioplasmic Forces'," in Thomas B. Roberts, ed., *Four Psychologies Applied to Education* (see Appendix B), which applies Steinerian principles to contemporary developmental issues.

21. Ian Stevenson, "The explanatory value of the idea of reincarnation," (ch. 5 n. 3).

22. Maya Pines, "Good Samaritans at Age Two?," *Psychology Today*, June, 1979, 66-77.

Chapter Ten

1. In Walter De La Mare, *Early One Morning in the Spring* (New York: Macmillan Company, 1935), p. 99.

2. Edward F. Edinger, *Ego and Archetype* (New York: J. P. Putnam's Sons, 1972), p. 11.

3. The following sources are useful in gaining a sense of the range of images surrounding childhood historically: Philippe Aires, *Centuries of Childhood* (New York: Vintage, 1962); Barbara Kaye Greenleaf, *Children Through the Ages: A History of Childhood* (New York: McGraw-Hill, 1978); and Peter Bennett, *The Illustrated Child*, (New York: G. P. Putnam's Sons, 1979).

4. Quoted in Herbert Read, *The Innocent Eye* (New York: Henry Holt & Co., 1947).

5. See Norman O. Brown, *Life Against Death* (Middletown, Ct.: Wesleyan University Press, 1959); and Elsworth Baker, *Man in The Trap* (New York: Macmillan, 1980), p. 69.

6. See Arthur Avalon, *The Serpent Power* (New York: Dover, 1974) for a description of kundalini; and June Wakefield, *Cosmic Astrology* (Lakemont, Ga.: CSA Press, 1968), p. 44, for a description of fohat.

7. Kerenyi, "The primordial child in primordial times," p. 50.

8. In F. W. Witcutt, "The child in paradise," Lecture No. 29, (London: The Guild of Pastoral Psychology, 1944), p. 12.

9. C. G. Jung, "The psychology of the child archetype," p. 178.

10. See Chapter 3 of this book for Jung's description of that dream.

11. In Edith Cobb, *The Ecology of Imagination in Childhood*, p. 90.

12. Ibid., pp. 90-91.

13. Bendit and Bendit, *The Etheric Body of Man*, p. 64.

14. For an excellent essay on this issue, see Ursula K. LeGuin, "The child and the shadow," in *The Language of the Night* (New York: Berkley Books, 1982).

15. Frank Haronian, "The repression of the sublime," *Synthesis*, 1, 1974, 51-62.

Index

Acupuncture, 70
Adolescence, 32, 76, 78, 90-91
Ahura Mazda, 58
American Journal of Diseases of Children, The, 19
ANABIOSIS: The Journal for Near-Death Studies, 19
Anandamayakosha ("bliss-body"), 73, 119
Angels, 3, 6, 14, 23, 71, 85, 93, 96, 118, 123-24
Animism, 142
Annamayakosha ("food-body"), 69
Apollo, 84
Archetype, 21, 36-37, 38, 43, 50, 77, 115, 118, 212; of the child, 84, 148
Artistic expression in childhood, 24-26, 94, 99, 106, 134
Arundale, George, 127
Asclepius, 84
Assagioli, Roberto, 41-42, 43, 50, 116, 118, 181. *See also* Psychosynthesis.
Astral field. *See* Emotional field.
Atlantis, 58
Atman, 47, 48, 74
Atman project, 47, 110, 189

Atman project, The, (Wilber), 105
Aura, 43, 69
Aurobindo, Sri (*see* Ghose, Sri Aurobindo)
Autism, 139-140
Autobiography of a Yogi (Yogananda), 20

Bailey, Alice, 141
Bardo, (after-death state), 105
Behaviorism, 2, 107, 137
Belief systems, 85, 88-90
Bendit, Laurence and Phoebe, 77, 85, 141, 149
Bernbaum, Edwin, 59, 61
Bickerton, Derek, 92
Bioenergetics, 131
Black Elk, 20-21, 37-38, 50, 82, 119
Blake, William, 1, 4, 14
Blavatsky, Helena Petrovna, 57, 68
"Body up" development, description of, 5-6; necessity for, 7-8; and contemporary psychology, 8; and non-ordinary experience, 9; and theories of religious development, 14; and childhood distortions, 21; and deep

Index

Moral development, 143
Moreno, Jacob, 93
Morphogenetic fields, 69, 184
Mother-child unity (symbiotic
  or fusion consciousness), 5,
  6, 9, 29, 50, 105, 110, 111,
  114; and Neumann's
  uroboros, 61; and Wilber's
  pre/trans fallacy, 103
Mother, The (disciple of Sri
  Aurobindo Ghose), 16, 50
Mount La Salette, 112
"Music-making children" of
  Ghana, 92
Myelinization, 34, 179
Mystical experience, childhood
  vs. adult, 17-18, 105-07
Mythology, 52-62; 84-85

Near-death experience (NDE),
  18-20, 50
Neotony, 94
Neumann, Erich, 60-61, 94,
  110, 115
"New-age" parenting,
  distortions in, 131, 149
Nietzsche, Friedrich, 147

Oaklander, Violet, 137
Observing self, 72
"Ode: Intimations of Immor-
  tality from Recollections of
  Early Childhood" (Words-
  worth), 3, 4
Oedipal crisis, 56
On Children and Death
  (Kübler-Ross), 23, 29
Open ground (Welwood),
  45-46, 74, 119
Oppenheimer, J. Robert, 94
The Original Vision
  (Robinson), 17
The Origins and History of

Consciousness (Neumann),
  60
Otto, Rudolf, 4

Paradise, 61, 103; exile from,
  7, 53, 57, 59, 81
Parapsychology, description of,
  28; telepathy in childhood,
  28-29, 115; precognition in
  childhood, 29; clairvoyance
  in childhood, 29-30; psychokinesis in childhood, 31-32;
  relation to etheric-emotional
  fields, 77-78. See also Psychic perception.
Parenting, 127-33; use of fairy
  tales, 130, 192; use of art
  activities, 130; effect of
  thoughts and intentions on
  child, 131-32. See also
  Family.
Participation mystique, 115
Peak experiences, 15-18, 80,
  106
Pearce, Joseph Chilton, 6, 31,
  89, 115
Pecci, Ernest, 139
Perseus, 54-55, 61
Persian mythology, 58
Personal development. See Ego
  development.
Personal ground (Welwood),
  45-56
Personality, 37, 68, 75-76,
  77-78, 80, 108-09, 116
"Peter Pan Syndrome," 95
Peterson, James, 30-31, 42, 50,
  116, 122
Physical vehicle (body), 66-67,
  68-69, 75, 147
Piaget, Jean, 9, 144; preoper-
  ational thinking, 9, 116-17,
  142; and religious develop-

200

ment, 13; and esoteric psychology, 76; vertical décalage, 110

Picasso, Pablo, 94

Plato, 58, 79

Poltergeist phenomena, 32, 42, 77-78, 122

Pope, Alexander, 145

Portrait of the Artist as a Young Man (Joyce), 94

Prana, 69

Prenatal consciousness, 108, 110-11, 179-80

Prepersonal consciousness, 103, 109, 110-11, 114-15; and Wilber's model, 47; and imaginary companions, 121

Pre/Trans Fallacy, 48, 102-111; usefulness of, 103, 111; description of, 104; limitations of, 104-5, 111, 189; and cultural development, 182

Primal scream therapy, 96

The Princess and the Goblin (MacDonald), 62

Proust, Marcel, 94

Psalm 137, 59

Psychic Children (Young), 123

Psychic perception, 27-32; closing down at age seven, 78; negative features of in childhood, 129-30. *See also* Parapsychology.

Psychoanalysis. *See* Freudian psychology.

Psychodrama, 93-94

Psychokinesis. *See* Parapsychology.

"Psychology of the Child Archetype" (Jung), 84

Psychosis, 115, 121, 139

Psychosynthesis, 41-44, 97

Psychotherapy, child, 137-140

"Puer aeternus," 95, 148

Quadrinity Process, 97

Radiant Student Project, The (Canfield and Klimek), 43-44

Ramakrishna, 16

Rank, Otto, 53, 55

Reich, Wilhelm, 96, 131, 148

Reincarnation, 23, 24; purpose of, 7, 81; and childhood memory, 64-65, 80; historical prevalence of, 79; theosophical view of, 79; and Tibetan Buddhism, 79-80, 107; explanatory value of for developmental psychology, 141-42

Religious cults, 187

Religious development, childhood, 13, 23, 132-33

Religious Experience Research Unit (Robinson), 17

Remembrance of Things Past (Proust), 94

Repression of the sublime, 150

Retarded children, 140

Robinson, Edward, 17-18, 26-27, 119, 129

Rolfing, 131

Rolland, Romain, 176

Round Table Foundation, 100

St. Augustine, 87-88

St. Catherine of Siena, 14

Salinger, J.D., 12

Sandtray therapy, 40, 137

Sanskaras, 79

Schactel, Ernest, 4

Schizophrenia, childhood, 121, 139-40

About the Author

Thomas Armstrong is an adjunct faculty member at several Northern California schools including the California Institute of Transpersonal Psychology, John F. Kennedy University, the California Institute of Integral Studies, and Rosebridge Graduate School. He is author of a book for teachers of special education and has published several articles on learning and child development. Currently he is director of Latebloomers Educational Consulting Services, an organization dedicated to providing alternative paradigms for children and adults who have been labeled "learning disabled."

QUEST BOOKS
are published by
The Theosophical Society in America,
a branch of a world organization
dedicated to the promotion of brotherhood and
the encouragement of the study of religion,
philosophy, and science, to the end that man may
better understand himself and his place in
the universe. The Society stands for complete
freedom of individual search and belief.
In the Theosophical Classics Series
well-known occult works are made
available in popular editions.

These Quest books are also available—

The Family Unconscious
By Edward Bruce Taub-Bynum
The collective unconscious and how it affects the
members of a family.

Spirals of Growth
By Dwight Johnson
The developmental potential within humanity from infant
to seer.

The Theosophical Publishing House
306 West Geneva Road
Wheaton, Illinois 60189